ONE SIZE DOESN'T FIT ALL

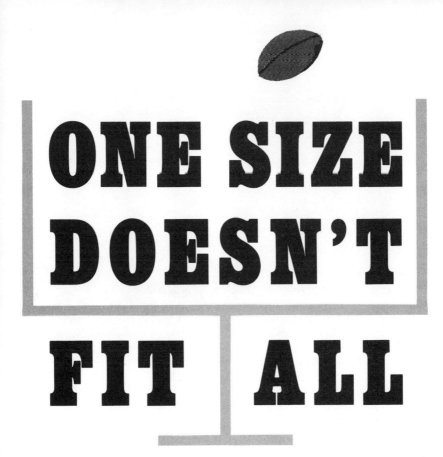

ONE SIZE DOESN'T FIT ALL

JOHN MADDEN

WITH DAVE ANDERSON

VILLARD BOOKS · NEW YORK · 1988

All rights reserved under International and Pan-American
Copyright Conventions. Published in the United States by
Villard Books, a division of Random House, Inc., New York,
and simultaneously in Canada by Random House of
Canada Limited, Toronto.

Library of Congress Cataloging-in-Publication Data

Madden, John, 1936–
One size doesn't fit all.

1. Madden, John, 1936–   . 2. Sportscasters—
United States—Biography. I. Anderson, Dave. II. Title.
GV742.42.M33A3 1988   070.4′49796′0924 [B]   87–40577
ISBN 0–394–56313–1

Book design by The Sarabande Press

Manufactured in the United States of America
9 8 7 6 5 4 3 2
First Edition

CONTENTS

CONTENTS

ONE SIZE DOESN'T FIT ALL

HOW'S THE BUS?

It never occurred to me that the Maddencruiser would create this much commotion. The only reason I ever thought about traveling on my own bus instead of by train was convenience. Being able to go when I wanted to. Being able to arrive when I wanted to. But now, wherever I am, most people don't even ask how my wife Virginia is. Or how our sons Mike and Joe are. Or how the Bears look. At least not right away.

The first thing most people ask me now is: "How's the bus?"

Hey, it's almost like the bus is a new member of the family. You know how people will see an infant wrapped in a blanket and say, "Oooh, there's the baby"? People do that when they see the bus. It's got MADDENCRUISER in small blue letters near the door and in big red letters on each side of the roof. I didn't want any identification on the bus, but Greyhound originally wanted to put a big photo on the side—they wanted it to be me breaking through a window, the way I broke through the paper wall on the Miller Lite commercials. So we compromised on the lettering.

At a quick glance, it looks like just another normal Greyhound bus, but a trucker sitting up in his cabin is about eye level with the big red letters on the roof. One day we were riding down the New Jersey Turnpike when a trucker in the next lane started waving at me. I could see him talking into his CB, so I turned on our CB.

"Hey, John, this is Muggsy. How's the bus?" he said. "I'm a big Giants fan. Season tickets. Section two-eleven, row seven, seats one, two, three, four."

Another time I was in Green Bay with Forrest Gregg, then the Packers coach, now the coach at SMU. We were in his office, talking football, when he suddenly looked beyond me out the window.

"There's the bus," he said.

When we were through, Forrest, like everybody else, wanted to take a tour. Often it's parked outside a stadium or outside a hotel where an NFL team is staying, and literally hundreds of football people have come up for a guided tour. Players, coaches, club owners. One day outside Three Rivers Stadium in Pittsburgh, the Steelers' owner, Art Rooney, climbed up the steps, glanced at the chairs and couch up front, checked out the kitchen and the shower, walked through to the big bedroom in the back, turned around, and looked at me with that Irish twinkle in his eyes.

"Good thing your roots didn't miss that boat coming over from Ireland," he said.

But hey, this book isn't all about the bus. Although you might say the bus is a vehicle for this book. I don't read as many books as I'd like to, but years ago I read John Steinbeck's *Travels with Charley*, a great book about his driving all over the United States in a camper with his bluish-gray French poodle. Ever since, I've wanted to do what John Steinbeck did—really get to know this country and its people a little better. Back when I was coaching the Oakland Raiders for ten seasons, I remember thinking the same thing. Every other week we'd travel to New York, to Denver, to Chicago, to San Diego, to Washington, to wherever, but all I ever did was arrive at the airport, get on a bus to the hotel, stay overnight, get on a bus to the stadium for the game, get back on the bus to the airport, and fly home.

As a coach, I traveled all over the country, but I had no *experiences*. And I think too many Americans are like that. When they take a vacation, they go to Europe or the Orient instead of really seeing their own country. Even when they travel in the United States, they usually just go from airport to airport. They never travel on the ground.

In the years when I traveled by train doing NFL games for CBS, I couldn't get off at every stop. But people certainly got on. Talking to some of those people, I got a feeling of what it was for them to live in Iowa or Mississippi or wherever. It made me want to spend time in those places. Now I can. I can stop when I want, I can change my route, I don't have to rush.

Traveling is something that almost everyone is interested in. Most people either have done it or want to do it. Either way, they like to hear about different places.

What's New York like? What's little Van Horn, Texas, like?

But mostly, this book is about what *I'm* like. My first book, *Hey, Wait a Minute (I Wrote a Book!)* was basically about broadcasting CBS games, riding trains, doing Miller Lite commercials, and having been the Raiders' coach. *One Knee Equals Two Feet* was about football players and coaches. And the title of this book, *One Size Doesn't Fit All*, sums me up. I got the idea in a hotel where a complimentary white terry-cloth robe was hanging behind my bathroom door. "One size fits all," the label read. But hey, that robe was too small for me. One size definitely *doesn't* fit all. That's one of the most important things I've learned along the way. Everyone's different. I know *I* am.

Not that I'm hard to please. I'm not nearly as fancy as my bus. I don't like fancy clothes. I don't like fancy food. Just let me wear a sweat suit and sneakers to a real Mexican restaurant for nachos and a chile colorado. That's my idea of a big night—not putting on a tie and hard shoes to go where they serve nouvelle salmon with strawberry sauce.

I love poker games. I love to just hang out. I never go to the movies or the theater. I'm not even big on music, unless it's Willie Nelson, the country-and-western singer I got to know when he used to come to Raiders games. Early in 1979, after I had stopped coaching, Willie invited Virginia and me to his concert at Stanford Stadium.

"Sit backstage," he said.

I thought backstage meant behind the curtain. But when we got there, we were sitting right up on stage, on the side. In the middle of the concert, Willie looked over at me and grabbed the microphone.

"And now," he said, "our next singer will be the former coach of the Oakland Raiders, John Madden."

All of a sudden the spotlight was on me, and I was on the spot. I had to go up there and sing.

" 'Amazing Grace,' " Willie said. "John's going to sing 'Amazing Grace.' "

I didn't know all the words, but I got through it. About a year later Willie invited us to another concert in the Oakland Coliseum, but this time I was ready. I got a tape of "Amazing Grace" and I learned the words. Then, when Willie sang "Amazing Grace," I thought I was in the clear. But he did it to me again.

"John Madden," I heard him say, "c'mon up here and sing 'Yellow Rose of Texas.' "

Naturally, I didn't know all the words to that one either.

Growing up in Daly City, just across the San Francisco city border, the only time I turned on the radio was to listen to a ballgame. About the only time I turn on the radio now is to listen to a ballgame, or to a sports talk show or the news. That's why I always listen to the AM stations, never to the FM stations. I don't want music. I want to know what's going on.

I'm lucky. I'm a football guy. My life revolves around the football season. From the time I was a little kid, I've always had a football season. As a player. As a coach. And now as a broadcaster. I'm doing what I love and I love what I'm doing.

When I'm in the CBS booth on Sunday afternoons, I wear my blue blazer with a shirt and tie. Other than that, I don't have to get dressed up to go to work every day. If I had to do that, I'd hate it. But now I get paid for what I've done all my life—talking football. And when I'm not talking football on CBS, I'm making a TV commercial or doing a radio show. It might not sound like much, but it can get hectic.

At first, I tried to schedule myself by the seat of my pants. When somebody would call me in June at our Danville, California, home and ask, "Can you do this commercial on August 2?" I'd say yes, but I'd never write it down. When I woke up on August 2, I wouldn't know what I was supposed to do. I tried to keep a calendar, but I kept losing it. Now when somebody calls to ask me to do something on a certain date, I don't say yes quite so quickly.

"Check it out with Sandy," I say now.

Sandy Montag is an account executive at IMG, the International Management Group founded by Mark McCormack, Arnold Palmer's lawyer. Sandy is a 1985 Syracuse University graduate with a degree in communications. He does some of my deals and on the bus, he's my traveling calendar. As nice as my bus is, when my wife, Virginia, wants to be in New York with me, she takes a jet. She doesn't want to rough it on the bus. So, on all my trips during the NFL season last year, Sandy was with me, sitting up front with Willie Yarbrough, my primary driver, or sleeping in a bunk.

"We'll be somewhere in Nebraska tomorrow morning when it's time to do your Z-100 radio show in New York," Sandy said one night. "I'll get you up."

The next morning, Sandy woke me. I squinted through the window curtains at a little white stucco restaurant, surrounded by empty fields where wheat and corn grew. In the gray dawn, I felt like I had landed on the moon.

"Where are we?" I asked.

"Potter, Nebraska," Sandy said. "The restaurant's not open yet, but you can use the public phone outside. Too bad the restaurant's not open. It must be a great place."

"How do you know it's so great?"

"Look at the name. Sandy's Café."

I threw on a sweat suit, squeezed into a pair of sneakers, and trudged to the phone. During the radio show I mentioned that it was so early, Sandy's Café wasn't even open yet.

"Too bad," I said. "It looks like the kind of place where they really know how to cook up an egg."

I thought it was around quarter to eight that morning. I was surprised that a little roadside cafe wouldn't be open by then. But it wasn't, so we got back on the bus and took off. I didn't learn until two weeks later that it was really quarter to seven.

"In that part of Nebraska," Sandy explained, "they're on mountain time."

"No wonder it was so cold there," I said. "I was freezing standing out there."

"It was about twenty above that morning," Sandy then told me.

"I didn't know that until now, either," I said.

Sandy's smart. He only tells me what I have to know, like it's time to get up to do the radio show. He doesn't tell me what I don't have to know, like it's only six-thirty and it's twenty degrees outside. But he's not so smart that he didn't pick up a nickname. One time when we were in Washington, D.C., for a Redskins game, Rudy Martzke, the *USA Today* sports television columnist, invited our CBS production crew out to his Virginia home. When we arrived, Sandy noticed an outdoor basketball hoop in the driveway. Sandy had always told us how he won two varsity basketball letters at Tenafly (New Jersey) High School, so he grabbed the basketball and took a one-hander from about fifteen feet. Didn't even reach the rim.

"Airball," somebody said. "Airball."

"Give me another shot," Sandy said. "C'mon, another shot."

Another fifteen-footer. Another airball.

Ever since, Sandy has been known as Airball. I was even tempted to title this book *Travels with Airball,* but then I realized that this book isn't only about my travels, any more than it's only about the bus. I think this book's as close as I can get to being about *everything.* Among other things, it's about pets and golf and broadcasting and having kids. It's about stuff I know and stuff I've seen. It's about when I was a kid in Daly City, growing up with my pal John Robinson, now the Los Angeles Rams' coach, and it's about how I wish the world would go by what sports goes by—somebody's record.

John Robinson always reminds me about the time I "threw" a home run. Other baseball players hit a home run, but I threw one.

I was a senior at Jefferson High School in Daly City, the catcher on the baseball team. We were playing Sequoia High School in Redwood City and John, who went to Serra High School in San Mateo, had come down just to watch the game. With nobody on base, one of the Sequoia batters struck out. But the pitch was in the dirt. I kept the ball in front of me and as it rolled a few feet in front of home plate, the batter took off for first base. I grabbed the ball but I thought, hey, let him go, make him run, then whoom, I'll throw him out. I let him go and then whoom, I threw the ball over the first baseman's head. *Way* over his head. Way down the rightfield foul line and down a hill. By the time the rightfielder got the ball, the batter had rounded the bases.

"You threw a home run," I heard John yelling. "You threw a home run!"

If anybody wants to check that out, it's on my record. That's one thing about playing and coaching. You have a record. Yards gained. Batting average. Wins and losses. I just wish everybody we deal with in the real world had a record that anybody could check. If you hire a lawyer to defend you in an auto accident case, do you have somebody who's 31–1 in auto accident cases or 4–28? Nobody knows.

It's the same with a doctor. If you need a heart bypass, what's the doctor's record in heart-bypass operations—99–1 or 51–49?

If you hire an accountant to do your tax return, do you know how often his clients had to appear later for an audit by the IRS? If you go to an auto mechanic to fix your transmission, do you know how often his customers complain that the repaired transmission doesn't work either? Moving along an interstate highway in my bus, I think about things like that. I think about goofy things too, like the time I forgot to put a new supply of Diet Pepsi on the bus. I didn't realize it until I saw one of those big Pepsi tank trucks rumbling along in the next lane.

"Hey," I said, "you know how planes refuel in midair? Maybe we can hook up with that truck."

THE DEAL

On one of my first trips in the Maddencruiser, the Iowa cornfields were swaying in the breeze along Interstate 80 when I heard Sandy Montag whispering on the telephone up near where Willie was driving. Sandy had his right hand cupped over the receiver like he didn't want me to know what he was doing.

"He's available Tuesday, Wednesday, and Thursday," Sandy was saying. "Almost any Tuesday, Wednesday, and Thursday."

I thought, hey, what a guy, he's working on a big commercial for me and he doesn't want me to know about it until the deal is all set. You got to love a guy like that. But then I heard something else.

"No, he can't do it Monday," Sandy said. "He does the Monday night game."

He does the Monday night game. I don't, so *he* sure wasn't me. In that case, he had to be Al Michaels, at the time an IMG client who did do the Monday night game. And here was Sandy trying to sneak a deal for Al, on *my* phone, on *my* bus! I yelled and screamed, but I couldn't get too angry. After all, Sandy had put together the deal with Greyhound when I was thinking about traveling by bus instead of by train.

Ever since I stopped flying in 1979, near the end of my first season as a CBS announcer, I had enjoyed the train. I still do. But the Amtrak schedule didn't always fit my schedule.

During the 1986 season, I had to go from Denver to Dallas, but on Amtrak the best way to go from Denver to Dallas is to go through Chicago. To make it worse, the train from Chicago to Dallas doesn't run every day. So when I got to Chicago, I had to wait a day to go to Dallas. Then, if it was a late game in Dallas, I had to wait until the next day to get a train out. If it was an early game, I had to drive to Meridian, Mississippi, to get the train coming up from New Orleans on its way to New York.

I loved the trains and the people on the trains, but it just got to where I was spending too much time waiting for trains. And every so often I would read where the Amtrak service was going to be cut back even more, so I decided to think about another way of traveling.

Several years ago, CBS wanted me to do a pool shoot with Willie Mosconi and Minnesota Fats in Las Vegas between NFL games in Atlanta and Philadelphia. That's when I learned that you can't always get where you want to go by train, at least not when you want to be there. I checked the Amtrak timetables, frontwards and back-wards, but there was no way I could get from Atlanta to Las Vegas on a Sunday night, do the pool shoot, then take a train that would get me to Philadelphia by Friday night.

"I'd love to do it," I told Terry O'Neil at CBS, "but the trains won't get me there."

"Suppose we get you a bus," Terry said. "Maybe we can rent one of those buses that entertainers use. If we can get a bus, you can do it."

"Hey, that'd be great," I said.

It turned out to be Dolly Parton's bus. It had easy chairs and a couch up front, a kitchen area, a sink and a shower in the bathroom, two rows of bunks, and a big bedroom the width of the bus. When the game in Atlanta ended, the driver had the bus waiting. I got on, read the papers, watched television, and went to sleep. I got to Vegas in time for the pool shoot, did the show, got back on the bus and pulled up to the hotel in Philadelphia in plenty of time to visit the two coaches on Saturday, like we always do before a Sunday game.

So when I started thinking about an alternative to trains, I remembered that bus trip. And the twist to my traveling in the Maddencruiser now is that the idea was developed on a train ride.

I was going from New York to Los Angeles for Super Bowl XXI, after the 1986 season, when Elizabeth Brackett and a television crew from the *MacNeil/Lehrer News-Hour* boarded the train in Chicago to interview me. She asked about football and the Super Bowl and coaching and broadcasting. Then she asked why I was riding a train across the country, why wasn't I in a 727?

"I don't fly," I told her. "1979 was the last time I flew."

I explained that when I started taking commercial jets

to my CBS games in 1979, I developed claustrophobia, which hadn't bothered me when I was the Raiders' coach. As a team we always flew on chartered jets, and I could get up and walk around. On the commercial jets I couldn't do that. I wasn't afraid that the jet was going to crash. I just didn't like being cooped up in that metal tube. Late in the 1979 season I switched to taking trains.

"And now," I told Elizabeth Brackett, "I'm thinking of getting a bus. That gives me a little more control, because on the train you have to go by the schedule. I'm thinking of getting one of those buses that have the bed and the kitchen and all that stuff."

When that interview appeared on Friday, January 23, three nights before the Super Bowl game, George Gravley, the public relations director for Greyhound Lines, Inc., happened to be watching. He was at the Ramada Valley Ho in Scottsdale, Arizona, where Greyhound was negotiating a new labor contract. While the top Greyhound executives, especially Fred G. Currey, the new chairman of the board, were trying to hammer out a new contract with their drivers and mechanics, George had stayed upstairs in his room to take phone calls from the media.

"That particular day, the negotiating session ran long," George told me later. "I was still up in my room, watching the network news. Then I turned on *MacNeil/Lehrer.* As soon as you started talking about getting a bus, I wrote myself a note."

George went to dinner that night with Fred Currey and the other Greyhound executives, but they had more important things to talk about than putting me in one of their buses. The negotiations dragged through Saturday and into Sunday afternoon. While most of the nation was watching the Giants win Super Bowl XXI, the Greyhound executives were finalizing their new collective-bargaining agreement.

"We got it done at about halftime," George says. "We hardly saw any of the game."

The next day Fred Currey and George Gravley boarded a commercial jet to return to Dallas, where Greyhound has its corporate headquarters. During the flight Fred was reading the *USA Today* sports section when he noticed my picture in a Ramada Inn ad.

"Fred pointed to the ad and said, 'We've got to get this guy on a Greyhound bus,'" George remembers. "That's when I said, 'I'm glad you brought that up. John says he wants to travel by bus now instead of by train. We ought to give him a Greyhound bus.'"

The way George describes it, Fred turned and stared at him for about ten seconds without saying a word.

"Some executives would have taken ten weeks to make a decision on something like that," George says. "But in those ten seconds I could see that Fred was calculating the cost, what we'd get out of it, and how we'd go about it. After he took those ten seconds, he just looked at me and said, 'Let's do it.'"

At the time, I wasn't aware of Greyhound's interest. But a few days after that *MacNeil/Lehrer* interview appeared, I began getting letters from people who wanted to sell or lease me a bus, who wanted to drive the bus, who wanted to cook for me on the bus. And three or four weeks after I got home from the Super Bowl, Sandy phoned from New York.

"John, you won't believe this," he said. "Greyhound wants to give you a bus."

Sandy was right; I didn't believe it. Nobody was going

to *give* me a bus—at least not the kind of bus that I knew
I wanted.

"What's the catch?" I asked.

"All you have to do is give motivational talks to their
employees in major cities when you travel during the
football season. About twenty-five talks over three years.
That's the tradeoff. It's a three-year deal. They give you
the bus for three years. You give them twenty-five talks to
their employees in the three years. After three years, it's
your bus.

"That's all? No TV commercials? No ads?"

"Just the talks to the employees. The new owners at
Greyhound are more interested right now in boosting the
morale of their drivers and their other employees than
they are in putting you in commercials or ads. You don't
even have to pay for the gas. All you pay for is whatever
food and beverage you put on the bus, plus your telephone bill."

"It sounds good," I said, "but I'll believe it when I see
it."

I figured, Sandy's young, Greyhound is just setting him
up. He'll learn; the deal will fall through. Nobody is going
to *give* me a bus. But a few days later Sandy phoned again.

"I'm going to Columbus, Ohio, to see the Custom Coach
people," he said. "That's where the bus will be custom-
ized."

Sandy talked to Kirwan Elmers, the president of Custom Coach, Inc., the company that he and his father
started in 1955. Through the years, they've done buses for
Muhammad Ali, Dolly Parton, Clint Eastwood, Johnny
Cash, Barbara Mandrell, and Conway Twitty: my kind of
people. I didn't hear anything at first, but when I went to
Las Vegas for the Hagler–Leonard fight, Sandy arrived

with some sample swatches of the upholstering for the bus furniture.

"I like the soft blue and beige the best," I said.

I thought, hey, maybe this Greyhound deal is going to work out after all. But in a few days, Sandy was on the phone again. Fred Currey had begun to wonder if I was the right guy to do those motivational talks. He had seen me do NFL games for CBS, but he had never seen me talk to people in person. To reassure him, Sandy sent him a film of a talk I had given at a United Way function.

"Fred loved the tape," Sandy told me later. "It's a deal."

Now it was up to Sandy to turn the deal into the bus. Before he returned to Columbus to supervise the design of the interior, I reminded him, "Don't forget, a big bed and a big shower." One size, remember, doesn't fit all. I knew if I had those two things, all the other stuff would work. But Sandy and Kirwan Elmers were also able to put in six inches more headroom plus six inches more—let's say, *belly* room—in the dinette booth. That was just the beginning.

"It was like going shopping with somebody else's money," Sandy told me. "Greyhound gave us an open checkbook. They wanted it to be the best bus on the road."

If it's not, it's not Greyhound's fault or Sandy's fault. Just inside the door of the bus is a blue leather chair, facing forward. Behind it is the dinette booth, with two benches upholstered in soft blue and beige, each wide enough for two people. Behind the driver's seat is another blue leather chair facing to the right, then an upholstered couch that can seat four people. As you walk back along the blue carpeting, you come to the kitchen—a refrigerator across from an oven, a stove and a microwave, a coffee maker, a sink, and a four-slice toaster. There are several cabinets in a beige butcher-block wood for pots and pans. Then comes the big tiled shower, with a sink and a toilet. In the back, across almost the width of the bus, is a queen-sized bed. Six other bunks are scattered around. Some pull out of the wall. Some drop from the ceiling.

"On some trips," Sandy had told Kirwan, "we're going to have two drivers."

That created a problem. If a trip took more than ten hours, two drivers would share it in five-hour shifts. But when one driver was sleeping, where did he sleep without being disturbed and without disturbing anyone else? Kirwan decided to put the driver's bunk across from the shower, with just enough legroom for anyone to get by. That way, if I was sitting up front or watching TV in the big bed in the back, I wouldn't disturb the driver who was sleeping.

"We do about twenty-five buses a year now, and we've been in business for more than thirty years," Kirwan said. "But that driver's bunk in the middle of the bus is a real first."

Sandy also put in some toys—a TV up front, and another TV above the foot of the big bed, a VCR for each TV set, two commercial video-tape players, two stereo units, a small TV satellite dish on the roof, three telephones (two up front, one in the bedroom), a four-unit intercom, a loudspeaker, and a CB radio. And when Kirwan learned that we would be playing poker on the bus whenever we had enough people aboard, he put recessed poker-chip holders on each corner of the dinette table.

"That's another first," Kirwan said.

The overall cost was nearly $450,000: about $180,000 for the bus shell, and about $270,000 for the customized interior, much the same price as some condos. Other than that, the bus is pretty much like any other Greyhound bus. On a full tank of 165 gallons, it has a range of nearly one thousand miles. It weighs thirty-seven thousand pounds. It could go from my Danville home, not far from Oakland, to New York in about fifty-three hours, about nineteen hours faster than the Amtrak schedule that requires a four-hour layover in Chicago between trains. But that didn't surprise me. On a train ride once, Merle Haggard invited me into his personal railroad car.

"My buses are going to meet me in Chicago," he said. "They left San Francisco half a day after this train did."

Now that I had the bus, I thought Greyhound would provide different drivers whenever I made a trip, but Greyhound had a better idea. They invited their most experienced drivers to enter the First Annual Greyhound–Madden Challenge, to select my primary driver. Each driver had to have a minimum of ten years' experience with Greyhound, and an excellent safety record. For the drive-off in the Oakland Coliseum parking lot, Greyhound's four regional operating companies each selected two finalists:

Garet Bowling of Pinckard, Ala.
Larry Choate of Seattle, Wash.
Leonard Foster of Chicago, Ill.
Dave Hahn of Denver, Colo.
Willie Martin of Winston-Salem, N.C.
Robert Robinson of New Orleans, La.
Joe Williams of Chesapeake, Va.
Willie Yarbrough of Whittier, Calif.

Over two days, the drivers took a twenty-five-question written exam, went through a pre-trip check of their bus, drove along the Nimitz Freeway into downtown Oakland and back, took a test in a simulator bus, and drove a tight course marked by orange cones in the Coliseum parking lot. Then, one by one, I talked to each of them. I knew I wouldn't go wrong no matter who I picked. Each is a great driver and a great guy. But the more I watched Willie Yarbrough, the more I thought he would blend in the best with all the people he'd be meeting on our trips. He always had a smile on his face, always a bounce in his walk. As it turned out, each of the other seven drivers joined us for at least one long trip when we needed another driver, but Willie was the primary driver. Much to his surprise.

"When I entered the contest," he told me later, "I thought if I won, I would be your driver whenever you were in the Los Angeles area. I didn't realize I would be driving every trip."

Wherever we went, Willie had that smile on his face and that bounce in his walk. And wherever we went, Willie found himself to be a celebrity. On one of our first trips, the Pittsburgh Press and several Pittsburgh television stations interviewed Willie outside Three Rivers Stadium while I was inside watching the Steelers practice and talking to Chuck Noll, the Steelers' coach. Back when I was an assistant coach at San Diego State and Chuck was an assistant coach with the San Diego Chargers, we got to be friends. We even played "full-contact handball," as Chuck likes to say with his dry sense of humor. But when I was the Raiders' coach, the Steelers were our big rivals and our relationship cooled. I hadn't talked to Chuck for several years until I met him in the hallway outside his office about a week before the 1987 season opened.

"I hear you've got a bus now," Chuck said.

"It's a beauty," I said. "You've got to come outside and see it."

"What is it, a Greyhound?"

"Yeah, it's a Greyhound."

Chuck grinned. "John," he said, "you were *never* a Greyhound."

ON THE ROAD

n the bus, most of the time we're just out there on an interstate rolling along. And when we're rolling across Texas, we roll all day. One night, we left Tampa after a Bucs–Bears game, and the next day we were out on the flat, dusty plains of west Texas, where we could see towns miles before we got to them. We were on our way to Anaheim, Calif., for a Rams–49ers game the next Sunday, but on this Monday night the Rams were playing the Browns in Cleveland.

Up front in the bus I turned on our TV, but all I got was snow. Sandy tried the telephone. Static.

"That means we're in the middle of nowhere," I said. "But maybe we can find a restaurant with a TV. What'd really be great is a Mexican restaurant with the Monday night game on. Out here the game starts at eight o'clock, so let's keep driving until just before eight o'clock and hope there's someplace we can catch it."

On the map, we could see that Van Horn, Texas, was the next town. Pretty soon we saw its lights shining in the distance. Not many lights, but enough to know that had to be it.

As we took the turnoff, I looked at my watch. Ten minutes to eight. Just in time for the game, if we could find the right place to see it. Coming into Van Horn, population three thousand, we slowed down going along Broadway, its main street. Then we saw the sign:

MEXICAN FOOD

TV ROOM

We had lucked out. And it looked like a good place: white-brick arches out front, with a shiny red, 1929 Model A Ford on display in front of a white-brick building. I wondered if it might be too good to be true.

"Do me a favor," I asked Sandy, "go in and check it out. And make sure they've really got the game."

Within seconds, Sandy was back. "It's a nice restaurant," he said. "But even better, they've got a little room with four or five tables and a big-screen TV that's got the game." Perfect. This was Chuy's (pronounced Chewey's), run by Chuy Uranga and his wife Mary Lou, and it had some of the best Mexican food I've ever tasted. No margaritas, none of that fancy stuff—just Mexican food and beer. We had found a *good* place. I ordered machaca— shredded beef fried with onions, peppers, tomatoes, and a hot cheese sauce, with flour tortillas on the side. After the waitress took our order, Chuy himself walked over.

"I like your menu," I said.

From the way I talked about Mexican food, he knew

that I knew what I was talking about. When my machaca arrived, I dipped one of the tortillas into it and began eating.

"These are good tortillas," I said. "Where do you get them?"

"I've got even better ones," he said. "My wife just made some *special* tortillas. Let me get you a few."

"Ooooh," I told Sandy, getting excited, "now we're getting the real stuff."

When he returned with the special tortillas, Chuy sat with us and watched the Rams–Browns game. He knew his football. His son Paul is a football trainer at the University of Texas, El Paso.

"How far is El Paso from here?" I asked.

"Not far," he said. "You should be able to get the second half of the game on I-10 almost as soon as you leave here."

"I wish we could stay," I said, "but we better get going."

If we had known we were that close to El Paso, we probably would have kept rolling in the bus until we picked up the game on our TV, then stopped somewhere for fast food. Instead, we had our best night of the 1987 season. You can't beat real Mexican food in a TV room with the Monday night game. And when we got back on I-10, we turned on the TV and, boom, we watched the second half rolling through El Paso and Las Cruces, New Mexico. As soon as the game ended, I fell sound asleep. I didn't wake up until I felt the bus slow down and pull off I-10 into a truck stop for gas.

"Where are we?" I yelled.

"Blythe, California," Sandy said.

I had slept all the way through Arizona, but now I decided to get the morning papers. I put on a sweatshirt, sweatpants, and sneakers. Still a little sleepy, I was walking to the newspaper boxes in the truck stop when I noticed seven California highway patrolmen coming at me. Not one or two. Seven.

I thought, *Uh-oh, what happened? What did I do now?*

But the sergeant smiled. He introduced himself as a friend of Carl Marsh, another California highway patrolman who's one of my best pals. We talked for a while, then I picked up the papers and got back on the bus. I was pretty proud of myself. I had slept until I felt the bus stop. Or so I thought.

"No," Sandy said, "we stopped coming across the border from Arizona. The border patrol went through the bus and took our apples."

"Our apples?"

"All those New York apples we had. They wouldn't let us come into California with those New York apples."

"I never heard a thing," I said.

Whenever the bus is in New York City, it's kept in what Willie calls "its own room" in the Greyhound garage. It is literally locked inside an area just about big enough for it to fit. I usually do several NFL games in Giants stadium, just across the Hudson River from New York City, but I also do games in Philadelphia, about two hours away, and Washington, about five hours away. About a month before one of the Redskin games, Neal Pilson, the president of CBS Sports, asked Pat Summerall and me to appear at a CBS sports night in Washington for the Senators and Congressmen.

"You'll go to Washington in your bus, won't you?" Neal asked.

"That's the only way I go anyplace," I said. "Door to door."

I thought it was strange that Neal cared how I got there. In the television business, you're usually just told to be somewhere at a certain hour. You're never told how to get there. But as soon as Neal started smiling, I knew why he had asked.

"Can I go along for the ride?" he asked.

"Sure, you can," I said. "Anytime."

About two weeks later, Neal had another request. "Do you have room in your bus for another passenger?"

"Sure."

"Good," he said. "L.T. would like to go."

To football fans, L.T. is Lawrence Taylor, the Giants' linebacker. I knew Neal didn't mean Lawrence Taylor, but I thought he meant somebody around the office who was known as L.T. for short.

"Yeah, sure," I repeated. "Whoever you want."

"I'm talking about Laurence Tisch," he said.

"Wooooo!" I said. "Laurence Tisch—*he* wants to go on the bus?"

"L.T. definitely wants to go on the bus."

Laurence Tisch has been the president and chief executive officer of CBS since 1986, when he purchased 25 percent of its stock. He later sold CBS Records for $2 billion. That's right, $2 *billion.* Laurence Tisch is a wheeler-dealer who made millions in the hotel business. His brother, Preston Robert Tisch, was then the Postmaster General of the United States.

"L.T. wants to bring his brother too," Neal said.

"Hey, plenty of room," I said. "Plenty of room."

I liked the idea of Laurence Tisch, and his brother the Postmaster General, and Neal Pilson going to Washington on the bus. But hey, I didn't know what kind of food to put on the bus for them. When I'm on the bus with Sandy, or anyone else, we eat whatever's there or wherever we happen to stop. But now Laurence Tisch and his brother Bob and Neal Pilson would be on the bus and I don't know what food.

As it turned out, the NFL strike postponed the sports night in Washington, and when it was rescheduled later in the season, Laurence Tisch and his brother had other commitments.

When we weren't going to Washington, it seemed like we were always going past it on I-95 on our way to Tampa or New Orleans. One of the biggest culture shocks in America is to go from New York City to the Deep South, especially to Atlanta, where the pace is so much slower. Back when I first started going to restaurants in New York, I noticed the abruptness.

"Whaddya want?" the waitress would snap.

The first time I heard that, I thought, *What did I do to make her mad at me?* I took it personally. After a while, I realized that's how most waitresses in New York talk to everybody, so I gave it back to them.

"Yeah," I'd growl, "gimme some coffee and a Danish."

But whenever I went to Atlanta for a Falcons game, the whole world seemed to slow down.

"Good mornin', suh," the waitress would say with a smile. "How are *you* this mornin'?"

And she meant it.

I remember listening to the late Bear Bryant's call-in radio show, when he was still the University of Alabama football coach. All his callers addressed him as "Coach," like they had played for him. Even the women.

"Coach," I remember one woman saying, "I met you last year down here at the Catfish Pond restaurant."

"That's right," the Bear said. "My good friend Jimmy Duffy lives in your town. You say hello to Jimmy for me."

Bear knew somebody in every city in Alabama, every town. His radio show wouldn't have worked in New York or Ohio or Colorado or California, but in Alabama he had the perfect radio show and he was the perfect coach. In the years when I rode Amtrak, everytime I went from New York to Dallas the train went through Tuscaloosa, past Alabama's practice field with the tower platform where Bear Bryant used to stand watching practice. Up on the platform he had hooked a metal chain across the space to the stairway.

"Whenever that chain hit the pipe," says Ray Perkins, now the Tampa Bay Bucs' coach, but once an Alabama wide receiver under the Bear, "we knew he was on the way down to chew somebody out."

Riding by the practice field, people would look out the window and point to the tower. "There it is," they would say, "Coach Bryant's tower." For them, it was like looking at the Washington Monument. On the train, I couldn't get off to watch the Alabama team practice. On the bus, I can stop wherever I want or whenever I want. Like the time we were on the way to New Orleans for a Saints–Giants game. That afternoon, rolling down I-65 toward Mobile, I decided we'd stop at a restaurant, get some food to go, and keep rolling. We hadn't been down I-65 before, but soon we spotted an interesting sign:

CREEK FAMILY RESTAURANT

We didn't know it until later, but this restaurant in Atmore, Alabama, is owned by the Creek Indians, who live on a reservation nearby. There's a totem pole outside the sprawling red-brick restaurant, which features a country buffet. That day they had a spread of fried chicken, smoked sausage, catfish, roast beef, spaghetti, vegetables, and cornbread. We had arrived at an off-hour and didn't have to wait, so instead of taking the food on the bus, we decided to eat there. Soon we got to talking with Mike Lowery, the general manager, who runs the restaurant for the Creek Indians. Through the window I noticed a big gray building with towers.

"What's that?" I asked.

"Holman State Prison," he said. "See that pole? That's where the electrocutions are."

"Electrocutions of prisoners?"

"That's it," he said. "For his last meal, a prisoner gets a choice of whatever he wants from the prison kitchen or from this restaurant. Few weeks ago a guy picked this restaurant."

"What did he want?"

"Just a hamburger."

"With what?" I wanted to know. I mean, I was curious to see what a guy'd eat for his last meal.

"Just a plain hamburger on a bun."

"No catsup?"

"No catsup."

"No onions?"

"No onions."

"No pickle?"

"No pickle."

"Just a plain hamburger on a bun for his last meal?"

"Plain hamburger."

By that night, we were in New Orleans, where the French Quarter is always lively, but except for eating at the Gumbo Shop, I've never spent much time there. It's too honky-tonk for me. Right after the game, we were on our way to Dallas for a Thanksgiving Day game. To me, Dallas has always been a combination of a city trying to still be Texas and one trying to still be new. In the downtown area, I can never find my way around. There don't seem to be any landmarks, just a bunch of big glass buildings. The first time you go to Dallas, there's no place you just must see. (Except for the Book Depository area, where President Kennedy was assassinated. But that's a negative thing.)

In every other major American city, there's always something you must see, even if I haven't bothered to see them all. In Washington, it's the White House, the Capitol, and the monuments. In Philadelphia, it's the Liberty Bell. In Boston, it's the Old North Church. In Chicago, it's Michigan Avenue. In St. Louis, it's the Gateway Arch. In San Francisco, it's the Golden Gate Bridge. In Los Angeles, it's Hollywood. In San Diego, it's the zoo. In New York, it's a dozen things.

In Dallas, there's nothing to see except the people. But they're enough. They're friendly, gregarious, outgoing. They're just nice people. When we were staying at the Four Seasons in Las Colinas, before the Thanksgiving Day game, the people at the hotel learned that we couldn't return there for a turkey dinner because we had to leave for Washington right after the game. So they cooked a turkey for us. They even gave us extra dressing. As soon as we got rolling out of Texas Stadium, we preheated the oven on the bus.

"We'll leave it in for about an hour," I said. "Really heat it up."

When the turkey was ready, Bob Stenner, our CBS producer, who was making the trip with us, carved it like a chef. Everybody ate some and when we got up the next morning, everybody ate some more. By the time we got to Washington, only the carcass was left. That turkey was the best dinner we'd had on the bus all season. Usually we just throw some leftovers in the microwave—barbecued ribs or chili, or both. But one morning when we were leaving home in Danville, California, for a forty-hour trip to Green Bay, I got hungry after about two hours. In the refrigerator was a batch of ribs and link sausages that we had bought at Jimmy Layne's in San Leandro the night before for a poker game. As it turned out, there was no poker game, so we put the ribs and links on the bus. But now I was so hungry, I started eating them cold. Sandy couldn't believe it.

"Why don't you put 'em in the microwave?" he wanted to know.

"I'm too hungry," I said. "I don't want to wait."

"That's the most disgusting thing I've ever seen."

Disgusting, but still tasty, even cold. I learned something else on that trip, about how to back-time. Before every trip, Sandy and Willie checked the maps to figure how long it would take, then they back-timed it. On that forty-hour trip, counting the two-hour time difference, we wanted to be in Green Bay on Friday night, so we left home at seven on Thursday morning and got there about eleven on Friday night. Then we realized that when you leave California in the morning, you're on the bus for two full days, which feels a lot longer than leaving the night before and sleeping on the bus two nights.

"The next time we go from California to Green Bay," I said, "we'll leave about ten o'clock two nights before, instead of the next morning."

Green Bay is one of my favorite stops. It's the NFL's only small town, a city with only a ninety thousand population. But mostly I like Green Bay because of Lambeau Field, named for Earl (Curly) Lambeau, the Packers' original coach, who got an NFL franchise in 1921 after the

Indian Packing Company put up the money for equipment. That's how the Packers got their name. To me, Lambeau Field is the NFL's best stadium. It was built to watch football in, nothing else. Every one of its fifty-seven thousand seats is a good seat. Its grass is the best in the league. And more than anything else, it's not domed.

I don't know why, but the domed stadiums in Houston, New Orleans, Seattle, Detroit, and Indianapolis don't bother me. I don't like them, but they don't bother me. But the dome in Minnesota bothers me. And if Green Bay ever had a domed stadium, it would more than bother me. It would be sacrilegious.

Until the Vikings got to the 1987 NFC championship game, they hadn't been the same team since they moved into the downtown Minneapolis Metrodome in 1982. They had some pretty good teams, but they hadn't been the *same* team that played in Metropolitan Stadium in suburban Bloomington, especially late in the season in cold and snow. Back when I was coaching the Raiders, we were lucky. We went to Minnesota only once, to open the 1973 season. We lost, 24–16. But we were happy just to go there when the weather was warm. In those years, nobody wanted to go to Minnesota late in the season. But the Vikings don't have that advantage anymore. With the Metrodome, it doesn't make any difference when a team goes to Minnesota now.

Unless you're an opposing coach or a player, you don't know what it's like to go into another team's stadium when the weather is cold. Or worse, when another team's fans are on you.

I didn't realize how difficult that was until I went to Three Rivers Stadium in Pittsburgh with our CBS crew for a Giants–Steelers exhibition, just before the 1987 season began. When we got off the bus outside the Steeler offices, nobody was yelling at us. Nobody was even there. And when I walked out on the field, I thought, *This is really a nice stadium.* All the other times I'd walked out there, I never had time to look around. I was too busy trying to ignore all those names the Steeler fans were calling me and my players. Hey, it's not the stadium, it's the situation. If you go out there with forty-five guys who want to beat the hell out of their forty-five guys, it's a different deal than going with a TV crew.

But the best game the Raiders ever played was at Three Rivers, a 16–7 victory over the Steelers in the second game of the 1977 season. We had won Super Bowl XI the season before. We wanted to prove we were better than the Steelers, who had won the two previous Super Bowl games. And we did.

My problems in Three Rivers had begun in the 1972 playoffs, the "Immaculate Reception" game. We went ahead, 7–6, with only seventy-three seconds remaining. After the kickoff, Terry Bradshaw completed two passes that put the Steelers on their 40-yard line, but then he misfired on his next three passes. Fourth down, twenty seconds left. Our pass rush pressured Bradshaw into scrambling, then he threw a pass downfield toward his halfback, Frenchy Fuqua, who went for the ball with Jack Tatum, our free safety. The ball rebounded off one of them (and after all the films I've seen, I'm still not sure which one). Then the ball floated back toward the Steelers' fullback, Franco Harris, who reached down, caught it at full speed at our 42, and ran untouched into the end zone for a sixty-yard touchdown with five seconds showing on the clock. In the confusion, none of the officials immediately signaled a touchdown.

Under today's rules, it wouldn't have made any difference which player the ball rebounded off. But at the time, the rules stipulated that if the ball bounced off an offensive player (Fuqua), a teammate was ineligible to catch it; if the ball bounced off a defensive player (Tatum), then Franco Harris had made a legal catch.

After the officials huddled in the end zone, the referee, Fred Swearingen, hurried to the telephone in the first-base dugout that the Pirates use during the baseball season. Swearingen got the switchboard operator to connect him to Art McNally, who was sitting near a TV monitor in the press box with Jim Kensil, then the NFL's executive director. Art has always denied having used instant replay to determine whether the ball bounced off Fuqua or Tatum or even to determine if the television picture was "inconclusive."

Whatever their conversation, Swearingen popped out of the dugout and raised his arms. Touchdown.

On my visit to Three Rivers Stadium before the 1987 season, I was talking to Steve (Dirt) Dinardo, the head groundskeeper who had always harassed us when I was the Raiders' coach. I brought up the Immaculate Reception, and Dirt told me that when Fred Swearingen went into the dugout to get on the phone with Art McNally, he was standing there with the referees.

"The ref said, 'How did you see it?' " Dirt told me. "Then there was a pause and the ref said, 'That's how I saw it.' "

I don't know what Art McNally told Fred, but from what Dirt told me, I think it's reasonable to assume that during that pause Art said something like, "I saw the ball hit the defensive player," meaning Jack Tatum, meaning that Franco Harris's catch was legal. I don't know if Art had checked the instant replay on the TV monitor or not, but he had a TV monitor next to him. And what I could never understand about Swearingen's call, if he didn't rule it a touchdown right away, was how did he know to rule it a touchdown later?

When we got back to Oakland after that game, I had a lip reader look at a video tape of Art McNally talking to Swearingen on the phone. But on the tape Art was too far away for the lip reader to tell anything.

Losing that game still rankles me. It always will. Some people try to console me by saying, "Forget it, John, it's just a game." But when you're in the arena, like I was when I was coaching, it's not just a game. It's your life.

But winning or losing a game isn't my life now. Analyzing a game on television is. Standing there talking to Dirt Dinardo in the middle of Three Rivers Stadium that day, I took off a hat I was wearing—and when I realized what the hat stood for, I had to laugh. In the Steeler offices earlier, somebody had handed me a black baseball cap with "Steelers" in gold on it. And here I was, the coach who hated the Steelers, the coach the Steelers hated, wearing a Steelers cap.

If that wasn't proof enough that my life is different now, after the Giants–Steelers game the next night, I had proof positive.

Back when I was coaching, I always had trouble getting to sleep after a game. I'd toss and turn, trying to think what I should've done or what I shouldn't have done. But that night in Pittsburgh, the game ended so late we decided not to return to New York on the bus until the next morning. We stayed in a hotel. I hadn't won *or* lost, but I couldn't get to sleep. I kept thinking about an idea that came to me when Pat Summerall did a promo for the

United States Open tennis championships that CBS would be showing the next week.

"They ought to have a tennis tournament for nose tackles," I had suggested. "And let tennis players be nose tackles."

By the time I went to bed, my head was spinning with all kinds of other tournaments. Linebackers would switch with race-car drivers. Imagine Lawrence Taylor zooming through a turn at the Indianapolis Speedway, or Darrel Waltrip playing linebacker for the Bears. Golfers would switch with pro wrestlers: Jack Nicklaus and Arnold Palmer against Greg Norman and Seve Ballesteros in a tag-team match; King Kong Bundy and Hulk Hogan playing golf. Jockeys would switch with basketball players: Angel Cordero, Jr., at center for the Lakers, while Kareem Abdul-Jabbar rides at Santa Anita. And pool players would switch with marathon runners: Minnesota Fats and Steve Mizerak running the marathon, and the runners playing pool.

I've always got little games going in my head, especially when I go over to the KSFO radio studios in San Francisco and stop at Enrico's for lunch.

I sit outside in the sidewalk café, across the street from the porno film store. One day a few years ago, I started checking out the people on the sidewalk in front of the store. Who went in and who went by. After a while, I could pick out the guys who were going in and the guys who'd pass by. It got so I could pick nine out of ten. And if I was sitting with somebody, I asked them to watch with me.

"See that guy?" I'd say. "He's going in."

Sure enough, he'd go into the store.

"But that guy," I'd say, "no way."

Sure enough, he'd keep on walking. Anybody who was with me thought I must have had a scouting report on these guys, but I didn't. It was just a matter of how they approached the store, which was the fourth door down from the corner. If a guy came up the hill, turned the corner, and walked in the middle of the sidewalk or on the outside of the sidewalk, he was sure to keep going. If the guy turned the corner and walked tight along the buildings, he was going in. Just before he went in, he always looked around like he was about to keep walking, then he darted in.

Coming out, guys acted just the opposite. Coming out, they walked out into the middle of the sidewalk as quickly as possible so nobody would suspect them of having been in there.

I think I'm able to read people in San Francisco better than I can other places. I grew up in Daly City, just across the city line, and now we live in Danville, east of Oakland, so for me a 49er game is a home game. Just because I'm from California, some people think I'm laid back. Hey, not me. I'm from the Bay Area, I'm from northern California, not southern California. In the Bay Area, we don't drop the buttons and hang the gold like Los Angeles guys do. When the Raiders were in Oakland, they had great fans, noisy fans. But if you watch a Raider game at the Los Angeles Coliseum now, it's quiet. Those people sit at a game and say, *OK, show me.* Then if you do show them, they say, *That's nice.* They get up and leave because they're bored.

California is really two different states, if not two different states of mind. But the bus makes it easy for me to go from one to another. By the time the Maddencruiser got a rest after Super Bowl XXII, it had 57,826 miles on it. And maybe the same number of laughs.

On one of our late-season trips, going home to California after an Eagles–Jets game at Giants Stadium, we were rolling through southwestern Nebraska on Interstate 80 when it was time for the Monday night game. We turned off at an exit for Sidney, a farm town of about six thousand about 165 miles from Denver, and started looking for a restaurant with a television set. We spotted a steak house, but after Mike went into check it out, he came back shaking his head.

"The only TV set," he said, "is in the bar."

Nothing against bars with TV sets, but I've learned that for me, a bar usually isn't the best place to watch a football game. Too noisy.

"Driving in here," Mike said, "I saw a TV set in the Tastee-Freez."

As it turned out, it was a black-and-white set. "Our color set," the owner, George Nolde, told us, "is being repaired." I ordered a soft taco, a bowl of chili, a strawberry sundae and a root beer, then I sat back to watch the Cowboys–Rams game. But just around that time George's wife, Evelyn, happened to call and George told her that we had stopped in to watch the game.

"His bus," George said, "is right outside."

I didn't realize it then, but Evelyn hurried over to where the Sidney High School basketball team had just finished practice. By the time my strawberry sundae arrived, so had the entire basketball team in their white-and-red jackets along with Jim Eberly, their coach. I signed autographs, then the football coach, Mike Mitchell, and his wife, Vicki, stopped by, along with a reporter from the Scotts Bluff newspaper.

"We're Bronco fans," one of them said with a smile. "We used to hate you when you were the Raiders coach."

But now they had gathered at a Tastee-Freez to watch me finish a strawberry sundae. Never underestimate the power of a chalkboard and a bus.

NO "ON" SWITCH

Before an NFL season I never seem to know which team will win the Super Bowl, but I do know which team will *not* win it. For whatever reasons, the team that won it the previous season has no chance. Murphy's Law takes over. Whatever can go wrong, will go wrong.

The New York Giants learned that. The Chicago Bears learned that. Every Super Bowl champion since the 1978–79 Pittsburgh Steelers learned that. Always the hard way. It's never any one problem. It's always an accumulation of everything, beginning with injuries. One reason any team wins the Super Bowl is that its best players have stayed healthy. But the next season, they're a year older. They're not only more susceptible to serious injury but they've run out of luck in avoiding serious injury. Ask the Giants, who lost Phil Simms with a damaged knee and Lawrence Taylor with a hamstring pull. Ask the Bears, who lost Jim McMahon with a damaged rotator cuff the year before.

Another factor is overconfidence. Now that the players are wearing Super Bowl rings, they *try* to be humble, but subconsciously, they think they're better players than they really are. They think they can just turn on their Super Bowl electricity whenever they want. Then they discover there's no "on" switch for that.

I can't think of any Super Bowl champion team that didn't reach the climax of its season in the Super Bowl itself. After that, there's a natural letdown. But in training camp, the team will try to resume at that same high point. When I watched the Giants struggle to beat the Steelers, 26–20, in their last exhibition game before the 1987 season began, I had the feeling that the Giants were trying too hard to start off at the same high level where they had ended up. It was understandable. They wanted to play well in their season opener against the Bears in Chicago, but they had forgotten what every Super Bowl team seems to forget: that it took them sixteen games and two playoff games to climb to that Super Bowl level.

I'm not being critical of the Giants or the Bears, or of any other Super Bowl team that was unable to repeat. I don't know that it's possible to go back to basics, to drop down to a lower level and then try to reach that crescendo again.

As soon as a team wins the Super Bowl, all its players are reminded every day that they're the Super Bowl champions, if only by the Super Bowl rings they're wearing. But with some teams, the reminders are more obvious: the six books that Coach Bill Parcells and his Giants players brought out; all the Chicago radio shows that the Bears had. In the early years, when a team won the Super Bowl, books and radio shows and shopping-mall appearances didn't exist, except for somebody like Joe Namath or Jerry Kramer. All this now contributes to the money factor that affects the players on a Super Bowl team.

"When we were winning four Super Bowls in five years," Terry Bradshaw has said, "we looked at every post-season game as a big-money game. Our salaries weren't that high then. The bonus money really meant something."

When the Steelers won their first two championships, after the 1974 and 1975 seasons, each player's post-season bonus came to $23,500 plus one fourteenth of his regular-season salary. After the team's second two titles, individual bonuses came to $32,000. But when the Washington Redskins won Super Bowl XXII, each player collected $64,000 in postseason bonus money. That might seem like a lot to most working people, but for some high-salaried players their Super Bowl money amounts to pocket change. Most, if not all, of it goes to Uncle Sam in taxes. The money incentive to win the Super Bowl just isn't what it once was.

That doesn't mean I think player salaries are too high in the NFL and other sports. There's a bundle of money out there, from television and radio, from ticket sales, from marketing. None of it is ever going to be handed back to the fans, you know that. So what we're really talking about is how all this money should be divided.

If the players don't get a big chunk of it, then the owners will keep it. I believe the players deserve their fair share. If that fair share comes to $2 million a season for

John Elway, the Broncos' quarterback, or to $200,000 for a steady but unspectacular linebacker, so be it. The fans buy tickets to see Elway, but they also buy tickets to see the team. And when the team wins, it's because all its players did their jobs. I've always thought of a good football team as if it were a good automobile. Just because the transmission is more expensive than the brakes, that doesn't mean it's more important. If you took the brakes out, how far would you be willing to drive the car?

There's another thing about sports salaries: a player seems to get more money either before he's earned it or after he's earned it. When the Seattle Seahawks signed Brian Bosworth for $11 million over ten years, nobody knew if he would really be worth $11 million or eleven cents. His money was on the come. And somebody like Brad Benson, the Giants' offensive tackle who blocked for Joe Morris in Super Bowl XXI, was rewarded with a $325,000 contract for the 1987 season, when he wasn't nearly so effective as he had been for $200,000 the year before. In most sports, your salary is seldom based on what you're really worth that particular season.

Ideally, the fairest way to pay pro athletes is to put up prize money, like golf tournaments do. If a touring golf pro like Jack Nicklaus doesn't win any money at a tournament, that's it, he doesn't get paid that week. In fact, not only does he not get paid, but it costs him money to pay his own expenses. If they ever paid football players the way they pay golfers, it would produce the damnedest NFL games you ever saw.

Still, in a team sport, it wouldn't be fair for the good players on a bad team to depend for their money on whether their team won or not. That's one reason why team sports are unionized. And that's why team sports have strikes, as baseball did in 1981, as the NFL did in 1982 and 1987. During the baseball strike and the 1982 NFL strike, nobody tried to play games. But a few weeks before the 1987 NFL strike, I was already so bored by all the labor stuff in the newspapers that I didn't realize the news value of a big story that Chuck Sullivan of the New England Patriots dropped into my lap. I was in the Metrodome to do a Vikings–Patriots exhibition game. Verne Lundquist and I were about to go on camera when Chuck looked into our booth.

"Hiya, John," he said, "how's everything?"

I was all hooked up. I couldn't even reach over to shake hands. All I could do was say, "Hey, Chuck, what's up?"

"We had our Management Council meeting Wednesday."

Just to make conversation, I said, "What happened?"

"We voted that if there's a strike, we're going to play the games with whatever players are available," Chuck said. "It won't be like 1982 when we went seven weeks without any games. We'll keep playing this time."

By now we were about to go on the air, so I waved to Chuck and he left. In my boredom with the labor stuff, I figured that what Chuck had told me must have been in the papers and I'd missed it.

"I was talking to Chuck Sullivan of the Patriots before," I mentioned during the telecast, "and he said that they had a meeting of the NFL executive committee, and they decided that they're going to play through the year. They said if the collective-bargaining agreement doesn't go through, if there's a strike, they're not going to not play. They're going to keep playing with whatever players they have."

I'm an analyst, not a newsman. As far as I was concerned, I was just bringing the viewers up to date on the strike situation, just telling them something they might have missed, like I thought I had. And despite all the strike talk, I didn't think the strike would happen. Several weeks earlier in San Francisco I had seen Gene Upshaw, the executive director of the NFL Players Association.

"If we could sit down with the Management Council for a couple of days," he said, "we could get it done right now."

Gene had been a Hall of Fame guard on my Raider teams, and I knew he wouldn't con me. But as the weeks dragged by, somehow a slit developed between the players and the owners. That slit became a gap. Then that gap got wider and wider. Even as the strike deadline approached, I kept hearing that the players would go out for a day, file an antitrust suit, then come back in. It turned out that they didn't file that antitrust suit until they had missed four weekends of games.

But when the strike began, I thought it would be over in a day. That shows you how much I knew.

On the Thursday of that first week, I was about to leave on our bus trip to Miami, where the Giants were scheduled to open the new Joe Robbie Stadium. But that afternoon the NFL owners called off that weekend's games. Those games were never made up. That empty Sunday Pat and I went into the CBS studios in New York and talked about the strike with Brent Musberger and Jimmy (The Greek) Snyder.

The following weekend, the "replacement" games began between teams of whatever free agents the clubs could sign off the street and whatever players crossed the picket line. It was exactly what Chuck Sullivan had told me would happen if a strike occurred. Pat and I were assigned to do the Cowboys and Jets at Giants Stadium.

Instead of thinking about football, I found myself thinking about the labor dispute. The day we went out to Long Island to watch the Jets practice, all I heard was how Mark Gastineau had got into a scuffle because one of his Jet teammates spat on him when he drove across the picket line. Or how Marty Lyons and Joe Klecko had crossed the line. Or how long the strike would last. Anything but football.

Hey, I'm a football guy. But this wasn't football. This wasn't what I do.

It's always been fun for me to visit a team's practice, and then talk to the coach and some of the players. But during the strike, the coaches didn't know what to say. They didn't want to demean the replacements, but they didn't want to say anything that their striking players might construe as an insult or that their owners might construe as disrespectful. The more I listened to all this, the more I realized that I wasn't having any fun and neither was anyone else.

The players didn't want the strike. The owners didn't want the strike. The networks didn't want it. And the fans sure didn't want it.

Fun or not, Pat Summerall and I had to do the Cowboys–Jets replacement game. In a way, I was in the same situation as all the NFL coaches. I didn't want those replacement games to be played. But the coaches had contracts that called for them to coach whatever NFL players the club owners provided. And as an announcer I had a contract to do whatever NFL games CBS televised.

When I get ready to do a regular game, it's more of a review than a learning process. I know 90 percent of each team's roster. I just check a few new players. It's like adding a few more drops of beer to a glass that's almost full.

But for the replacement games, it was like pouring beer into an empty glass. I didn't know any of those guys. Well, maybe two or three on each team, but that's all. For three weeks, I spent a lot of time putting together new names and numbers. That didn't bother me. I figured, hey, if we're going to do this game, let's do it right. But what *did* bother me was wondering who cared about these guys' backgrounds or what they had to say. Who really cared?

I knew I didn't care.

That's nothing personal against the replacement players. The ones I met were nice guys and they loved football as much as I do. But they weren't NFL players, and they would be the first to admit it. They knew, and I knew, that almost all of them would disappear as soon as the strike was over. Which they did. But when the real players returned, the season was out of sync. With all the money both the players and the owners lost, you just can't come back one day and say, hey, it's over now, everything is normal again. It doesn't work that way. Of all the people I talked to about the strike, Tom Landry, the Cowboys' coach, had the best explanation.

"The effect of the strike," Tom said, "was greater than anyone thought. You have to remember that football players are human beings with human feelings, not slabs of beef or robots. Something like a strike affects different people differently. When you try to put them back into a team situation, it's never as smooth as it was before."

Even without the strike, the 1987 season probably wouldn't have been so smooth for the Cowboys, who were on the downslide after having been on top for so long. In the NFL system, every team is going to have ups and downs. Even the Raiders struggled in 1987 after all their good years. Drafting at the bottom doesn't hurt you at first. But after a few years, if you don't get a good player in the first round, or the quarterback you're counting on doesn't come through, all of a sudden you're in trouble.

When the Raiders won two Super Bowls with Jim Plunkett at quarterback, Marc Wilson was their quarterback of the future. But when the future arrived, Marc didn't come through.

The same thing happened to the Cowboys, who groomed Danny White to succeed Roger Staubach at quarterback. White did the job, helping the Cowboys get to the NFC championship in his first three years, to the wild-card playoff his fourth year, and to a divisional playoff his sixth year. By then the Cowboys thought that Gary Hogeboom would succeed Danny, but then they decided that Gary wasn't the guy. After they traded Gary to the Indianapolis Colts, they started grooming Steve Pelluer, but they still seem to be looking for their next quarterback.

In the NFL, you can't win the Super Bowl without a prominent quarterback. Look at the quarterbacks who have been on winning Super Bowl teams—Starr, Namath, Dawson, Unitas, Staubach, Griese, Bradshaw, Stabler, Plunkett, Montana, Theismann, McMahon, Simms. Some of those quarterbacks are already in the Pro Football Hall of Fame. Most, if not all, of the others will be inducted, sooner or later. Of the new quarterbacks in the last couple of seasons, I like Jim Kelly of the Buffalo Bills the best. He's why I think the Bills have a chance to be one of the NFL's best teams. Maybe even a Super Bowl champion. Kelly is big, strong, tough. He projects that sense of command that only a quarterback can provide. In the NFL, no matter how good a running back is, he can carry a team only so far. In the NFL, you win the Super Bowl with a passer, not a runner.

As much as Eric Dickerson means to the Indianapolis Colts, as a running back he can take a team only so far, and never as far as a good quarterback can.

The way my CBS schedule broke during the 1987 season, I was in Los Angeles to do a Rams–49ers game when the Dickerson trade was developing. On joining the Colts he said, with a satisfied smile, "My strategy worked pretty good." His strategy was to get traded so that his new team would pay him the big salary the Rams wouldn't. He wound up with a reported $5.4 million over four years from the Colts, so his strategy certainly did work pretty good—his *financial* strategy.

But the Rams' front office never should have let the situation deteriorate to the point where they had to trade Dickerson.

"In professional football," John Robinson, the Rams' coach, told me that week, "you're always going to have contract squabbles. Players who want a better contract. Players who don't sign when they're drafted. Players who want to renegotiate their contracts. That's part of the business. And as a coach you have to cope with that. But this was the first time a player ever took that situation onto the field."

Dickerson, who was making $682,000 a year, gave the impression that he was so unhappy about the Rams' offer of $975,000 that he might not be able to put out 100 percent. In a Monday-night game in Cleveland, he didn't start for the first time in his Ram career. When he was put in, he skipped twenty-seven yards for a touchdown, but then he talked about having aggravated a sore thigh muscle.

Three days later, John Robinson announced that Dickerson "was physically and mentally unable to play" and put him on the inactive list.

That's when the situation got to the point where Dickerson, to get the contract he wanted, had to be traded and Robinson, to remain in command as the coach, had to trade him. But the Rams' front office never should have let it get to that point. That's easy for me to say. Back when I was coaching, I never had a salary problem with a player because Al Davis's greatest strength as the Raiders' managing general partner was to see a salary problem developing and solve it before it surfaced. Al would call a player in and give him a big raise almost before that player thought he deserved a raise.

"You got to pay the players," Al always said.

In a way, Al's thinking was a factor in the Dickerson situation. Eric resented Marcus Allen of the Raiders making $900,000. In his complaints, Eric also talked about how several other Raider players were making much more than several Ram players. Knowing Al, he must have enjoyed knowing that the Raiders' higher salary structure had been a factor in the Rams having to trade their primary attraction.

Even though the Rams were over a barrel, they put together a terrific deal. They got the Colts to trade Cornelius Bennett, the linebacker from Alabama they had been unable to sign, to the Bills in order to accumulate the draft choices the Rams demanded—three first-round choices and three second-round choices over the 1988 and 1989 drafts. If the Rams use those choices wisely, they have a chance to get well.

But at the time of the trade, the Rams were really hurt. Until the situation deteriorated, Dickerson was not one of those disliked players that every team is glad to get rid of.

His teammates liked him. His coaches liked him. And he was willing to carry the offensive burden.

As long as Dickerson was running the ball, the Rams' young quarterback, Jim Everett, had time to develop. Jim knew that the pressure wasn't on him, that he could hand off to Eric, that he was being brought along slowly, the way a young quarterback should be brought along. As soon as Dickerson was traded, and even though Charles White led the NFL in rushing, *boom,* the pressure was on the kid quarterback. And he wasn't ready for that burden. Now it's going to take Jim longer to develop than it would have if Dickerson were still in a Ram uniform.

In the NFL, everything about a team starts with its quarterback. That's why I think the rules should provide more protection for a quarterback. But whenever I bring this up in a conversation with football people, some guy always asks, "Do you want to put a skirt on a quarterback?" Hey, a quarterback doesn't have to prove to me that he's macho. If he wasn't tough, he wouldn't be a quarterback. Of all the players in a football game, a quarterback is more defenseless than anybody else. When he's passing, he's a sitting duck for any tackler who wants to take a shot. If a punter isn't allowed to be touched when one leg is in the air, I don't see why a quarterback shouldn't be protected when he's in the act of passing. He shouldn't be bounced around like a rag doll.

In the NFL, there are twenty-eight teams. But there aren't even twenty-eight good quarterbacks, much less enough to go around when some of the best quarterbacks get hurt, as they do each season.

When an injury takes somebody like Jim McMahon or Joe Montana out of the lineup, his team not only loses his athletic ability but it also loses his personality. McMahon's rapport with his teammates is well documented. Through the 1987 season and playoffs, the Bears had won twenty-eight of their last thirty games when Jim was healthy enough to start. Montana isn't quite so swashbuckling as McMahon, but Joe's quiet leadership permeates the entire 49er team.

Another way to reduce injuries, not only to quarter-backs but to all the players, would be to tear out the artificial turf. Falling on that is like falling on a throw rug in the street.

In my view, football should never be played on artificial turf, or worse, in domed stadiums. Football should be played on God's turf, grass, in the hot sun or in freezing cold, whatever comes up that day. The players should get their uniforms dirty, even a little bloody. They should sweat. Or they should be hopping around, trying to stay warm. That's football. You don't see it much anymore. But if you were watching the Bears' 26–24 win over the Packers in 1987 on Kevin Butler's fifty-two-yard field goal, you saw it. In the closing minutes of that game, Neal Anderson, the Bears' running back, didn't get up right away after a tackle. As he lay on the ground at Lambeau Field, one of our CBS cameramen zoomed in on a close-up of a chunk of grass as big as a golf divot jammed across his helmet, just above his face.

When that close-up appeared on the monitor in our CBS booth, I decided not to spoil it by trying to say something clever. To me, that scene was what Rembrandt would have painted if he were a pro football fan. I just stood back and admired it.

IN THE BOOTH

As an analyst at NFL games, the most important thing I do is tell the viewers what I honestly think about what's going on out on the field. For better or for worse—when a coach or a player is doing a good job, or when a coach or a player is not doing a good job. In or out of the booth, if I'm talking about NFL teams, I have to be honest with myself. I can't worry about being critical, even if it hurts somebody's feelings once in a while. During the 1985 season I mentioned that Dan Henning, then the Falcons' coach, had a "predictable" offense. Dan disagreed, saying he didn't think I had a right to say that because I hadn't seen enough Falcon games to know. And when Dan's quote appeared, my son Mike was concerned.

"You can't say stuff like that," Mike said. "Nobody's going to like you."

"But it's true," I said. "The Falcons do have a predictable offense. Run on first down. Run on second down. Pass on third down."

"Even so," Mike said, "you can't say that."

"If it's true," I said, "you can say anything."

Well, almost anything. You can't libel or slander someone. You can't say things that are in bad taste. But you can criticize or praise a coach's strategy, a player's performance, an official's call. To me, that's just being honest. I'm not a pretty face. I'm not a voice. I'm a pro football analyst. And my analysis is honest because it's a product of my experience in football and my preparation. Some people probably think that I just walk into the booth on Sunday and wing it. But it doesn't work that way. As soon as I leave the booth after one game, I start preparing for the next game.

I usually watch the Sunday night game on ESPN and the Monday night game on ABC, especially if those games involve any of the teams I'll be doing the following Sunday. During the next few days I try to read as much as I can about the two teams. I brush up on the uniform numbers of the players. I check the stats.

By the time Pat and I, along with our producer Bob Stenner and our director Sandy Grossman, visit both teams on Saturday, we're ready to ask questions. Back when I first started, I thought I'd learn more if we talked to the home team on Friday and the visiting team on Saturday, but I tended to forget some of the things I learned on Friday, so it's better to stuff both teams in on Saturday. That way everything is fresh in my mind. So is everything I've seen.

Some people assume that we go to a team's practice to watch its offensive plays. But that's not the main reason. For me, watching practice is important because it gives me an opportunity to see the players in their uniforms. Especially new players. I'm not talking about the numbers on their uniforms. After you do a team a few times, you know the numbers. It's more important to know what a player looks like in his uniform. During a game things happen so fast, I really don't have time to stop and think that Russ Grimm, the Redskins' guard, wears 68. But by watching Russ practice, I'm reminded what he looks like in his uniform. Russ is six foot three and 275 pounds—one of dozens of NFL linemen that size. But no matter how big or how small each player is, he's different. His body is different. His walk is different. His crouch is different. His run is different. I like to think that I'd be able to identify most NFL players from the booth even if they didn't wear numbers.

When practice is over, we always visit with the head coach for half an hour. We don't want his secrets; we just want some information that we can pass on to the viewers.

I really enjoy these sessions. Many were coaches when I was the Raiders' coach, like Don Shula, Tom Landry, Chuck Noll, and Chuck Knox. Or they were then prominent assistant coaches that I got to know, like Mike Ditka, Bill Walsh, Buddy Ryan, Dan Reeves, and Joe Walton. Or maybe one was an assistant coach who was with me somewhere, like Joe Gibbs was when we were at San Diego State together. Maybe another was on my Raider staff, like Tom Flores. Or one grew up with me in Daly City, like John Robinson, who was also on my Raider staff. The older coaches never hesitate to answer our questions, but sometimes a young coach will give me a guarded answer. Back in 1983 when Bill Parcells took over as the Giants' coach, they were about to open the season against the Rams.

"I'm a little scared telling you all this," Parcells finally said. "I know you're a good friend of John Robinson."

"I guarantee you, Bill, that I'm not going to tell another coach what you say anymore than I'm going to tell you what another coach says. The first time I ever do that with any coach, I'm through."

I was a little annoyed. But hey, Bill was a rookie coach. He didn't trust anybody. He hardly knew me. Now, we're good friends.

After our talk with the head coach, we like to hang out in the locker room with the players. We just have conversations, not interrogations. And if we didn't get a chance to look at game film before practice, we make sure we do before we leave to check the visiting team at their hotel. Visiting teams usually practice at their own complex on Saturday, take a chartered jet to the city where they'll be playing on Sunday, then ride chartered buses directly to their hotel. We stop by the head coach's suite, then talk to three or four players. All the players are helpful, but some are more interesting than others, like Jim McMahon of the Bears.

The night before the Bears played the Packers in Green Bay during the 1987 season, Jim was waiting for us in a small meeting room at the Paper Valley Hotel in Appleton, Wisconsin. He had his back to us, but I knew it was him.

Of all the players in the NFL, only Jim McMahon would be wearing black leather boots with silver buckles (riding boots, not cowboy boots), black leather pants, and a black leather jacket over a gray shirt with a skinny black leather tie. His hair was spiked up, he had sunglasses on, and he was on the telephone.

"Sushi," he was saying. "I hear you have good sushi."

He was making reservations at a Japanese restaurant. I'm sure the restaurant was highly recommended, but when I'm in Green Bay, when I'm in the Ultimate Small Town America, I prefer a good steak or a good bowl of chili. I wouldn't want to try a sushi restaurant there, but then I'm not the sushi type. Neither is Jimbo Covert, the Bears' 270-pound tackle, who happened to be there while McMahon was on the phone.

"You going to the sushi place with McMahon?" I asked.

"Sushi?" he said with disdain. "I don't eat sushi."

But whatever Jim McMahon eats on Saturday night, he knows how to play football on Sunday afternoon. He knows how to produce. Against the Packers the next day, the Bears were trailing, 24–23, with fifty-six seconds remaining. Boom, boom, two completions for forty-one yards, then Kevin Butler kicked a fifty-two-yard field goal as time ran out. Bears, 26–24. The week before, against the Kansas City Chiefs, the Bears were down by twelve going into the final period. Boom, a twenty-five-yard touchdown pass to Willie Gault and boom, a thirty-eight-yard touchdown pass to Gault. Bears, 31–28. And the week before that, in Tampa, the Bears were losing 20–0, when Jim came off the bench in his first appearance since surgery the previous December on his right shoulder for a torn rotator cuff.

"I just want to play the second half tomorrow," he had told me the night before. "Finish the game tomorrow, then start next week."

Jim thought the Bears would be in command by halftime. Instead, he had to win the game. He completed seventeen of twenty-four passes for 195 yards, including a six-yard pass to Neal Anderson. Bears, 27–26. Almost as soon as he came in that day, he reminded me of George Blanda when he was winning all those games for the Raiders in 1971 with last-minute field goals and touchdown passes. It got to the point where George believed he was going to win the game, then his teammates believed it, then all the people in the Oakland Coliseum or the opposing stadium believed it, and then even the opposing team believed it. As soon as George trotted onto the field, you could see the players on the opposing team drop their heads. They knew that George was going to beat them. That day, when Jim McMahon trotted onto the field in Tampa, the same thing happened. He believed he was going to win the game, then his teammates believed it, then all the people in Tampa Stadium believed it, and even the Bucs believed it. One by one, the Bucs players dropped their heads. They knew McMahon was going to beat them.

But what I really like about my Saturday visits is seeing the players as they are, sitting around the locker room, sitting around in a hotel. It's especially fun with somebody like Jim McMahon.

Here he was, that night in Green Bay, about to leave for a sushi restaurant in his black leather outfit with his black boots and his black leather tie. Instead of talking about the Packer defense, all he wanted to talk about was how his little son Sean had thrown up the night before.

"After he threw up, I took him into bed with me, figuring he'd sleep better," he said, laughing. "Then he threw up all over me and the bed."

In preparing to do a game on television, I never know where my best information will come from, so I try to talk to as many people as possible. The best information I ever got developed about three hours before a game. The day before the 1985 National Conference playoff between the Giants and the 49ers at Giants Stadium, I visited the 49ers at their New Jersey hotel. I talked to Bill Walsh and some of his players, but Joe Montana wasn't around. I'd always found Joe to be very helpful in letting me know little things. Hoping to see Joe in the locker room Sunday morning, I arrived at Giants Stadium earlier than usual. As soon as I walked down into the tunnel where the CBS trucks were parked, Chuck Milton, our senior producer, waved to me.

"Montana's here," Chuck said. "He's waiting for you in the 49er locker room."

Joe was one of only half a dozen 49er players already there. The rest of the 49ers would be along in about an hour. I poured myself a cup of coffee and sat down with him.

"What are you going to—" I started to say.

"I don't even know if I'm going to play," Joe interrupted. "I haven't thrown all week."

"What?"

"I tore my ribs, I can't throw the way I should. I don't know if I'll have anything on the ball."

"Are you going to play or not?" I asked.

"I think Matt Cavanaugh should play."

Nothing about Joe's ribs had been listed on the latest NFL injury report, but now he didn't think he should be starting. And when Pat Summerall and I did our opening, I talked about how Joe Montana was hurt and didn't think he should start.

As it turned out, Joe did start, and he played the whole game. He completed twenty-six of forty-seven passes for

296 yards. But the 49ers never scored a touchdown and the Giants won, 17–3. Maybe Matt Cavanaugh should've started.

That day, Joe Montana's doubts about himself created a story line, but as the game developed it was only part of the story line. Some broadcasters make a big deal of what the story line of the game is going to be, and then they try to justify that story line throughout the game. But for Pat Summerall and me, the story line develops during the game. If, say, John Elway of the Broncos gets hurt in the second quarter, that's the end of that story line. Now his backup is the story line. Or if Lawrence Taylor can't do much for the Giants because he's double-teamed or triple-teamed, Carl Banks might emerge as the story line. The idea is to recognize the story line when it appears, not try to insist on what the story line is supposed to be.

In the booth, I just try to be me, the same guy I was as a coach. On the sideline I moved around in my shirtsleeves. Unless it's really freezing, I'm the same way in the booth. In my shirtsleeves. Moving around. Swinging my arms. I once knocked Pat Summerall's headset off.

Pat's the best. No matter how excited I get, he always settles me down. And he has a knack for summing up a situation, whether it's something I've just said or something that's obvious out there on the field. Some play-by-play announcers will say, "That's right" or "It sure was" or they'll repeat what the analyst just said. But when Pat summarizes what I just said, he never uses the same words. And when I don't know what to say, he always does. Like one Sunday when a player blocked a punt with his groin and flopped to the ground in agony, and I just looked at Pat and shrugged.

"That'll make you cough," Pat said.

I laughed so hard I had to take my headset off before it fell off. But just as Pat knows to give me enough room to wave my arms in the booth, he also knows to give me enough room when I'm about to do a chalkboard diagram. I'm really bouncing around the booth then. I feel like I did when I was teaching at Allan Hancock Junior College or San Diego State, putting something up on the blackboard so all the students could understand it better. One of my proudest chalkboards was when I diagramed the loose zone defense that the Giants used against the Redskins in the 1986 NFC Championship game.

"In man-to-man defense," I said, "every defensive back and linebacker has a man to cover. But in a zone defense, players cover a zone or an area instead of a man. Usually you have three deep zones and either four or five short zones. But the looseness or tightness depends on the coverage in the four or five short zones. In a tight zone, those four or five players would go back eight to ten yards. In a loose zone, they'd go back twelve to fifteen yards."

Of the hundreds of chalkboards I've done, most people's favorite is the one they call "The Gatorade." In the closing seconds of the Giants' 17–0 victory over the Redskins in that NFC Championship game, I kept checking the Giants sideline to see if Harry Carson, their captain, was hovering near the orange Gatorade bucket. Every week during their winning streak, Carson had sneaked up behind Parcells and emptied the Gatorade bucket over him. With the Giants only two minutes away from going to the Super Bowl for the first time, I did a chalkboard over a shot of the Giants sideline as Carson stood near the bucket.

"You see, here's the bucket," I said. "Now Carson will come here. He'll get the bucket, come around here, come up here, find the coach and do the dump. Right in here."

When the game resumed, sure enough, Carson sneaked up behind Parcells and doused him. Parcells laughed, but deep down he didn't enjoy it. It's no fun getting splashed when you're not looking, especially in the chill of a late-season game. But being superstitious, he knew that if he didn't get splashed it meant the Giants had lost. He didn't want to risk that by telling Carson not to splash him any more. So he accepted the dousing. That wasn't his only superstition. When the national anthem was played, he always stood on the sideline exactly at the 50-yard line, with Carson to his left. And just before Harry went out on the field for the coin-toss, they had exactly the same conversation.

"What do you want me to call?" Carson would say.

"Don't ask me," Parcells would say with a grin.

Anybody who followed the Giants knew about those Parcells superstitions. But they didn't know about another superstition—his tuna-fish sandwich. On the third weekend of the 1986 season, we were assigned to do the Giants–Raiders game at the Los Angeles Coliseum. The day before, we talked to Bill at the hotel where the Giants were staying. Instead of meeting us in his suite, Bill suggested we go to the coffee shop. When a waitress came over, he glanced at the menu.

"I'll have a tuna-fish sandwich," he said.

His players would have chuckled. Bill's nickname is Tuna, because he's shaped like a tuna. So here was Tuna having some tuna. The next day, the Giants won, 14–9. We didn't do another Giants game until the seventh weekend. When we got to their Seattle hotel, Bill wanted to meet in the coffee shop again. This time he didn't even look at the menu.

"The last time we talked, I had a tuna-fish sandwich," he said. "I better order another one."

The next day the Giants lost, 17–12, but then they stopped the Redskins in a Monday-night game. The following Sunday they were to play the Cowboys at Giants Stadium, so we went over there Saturday to watch practice. Sandy Montag was with us, carrying a brown paper bag.

"What's in the bag?" I asked.

"Tuna for Tuna," Sandy said.

When we sat down with Bill in his office, Sandy handed him the tuna-fish sandwich. Bill took it, ate it, never said a word about it. After that, whenever we did a game at Giants Stadium, Sandy would stop at a deli for a tuna-fish sandwich. By then the Giants were really rolling. When they won the NFC championship, they had an eleven-game winning streak. Never mind the Gatorade; to Bill Parcells his tuna-fish sandwich had been just as important. The day before Super Bowl XXI, I was going to meet Bill at the Giants' hotel in Los Angeles, but first I had to see Dan Reeves in Costa Mesa, where the Broncos were staying. On the ride down there in our van, Sandy was fidgety.

"Do we have time to stop after we see Reeves?" he said.

"Stop for what?" I said. "After we see Reeves, we'll get back in the van and go to see Parcells."

"No, we've got to stop," Sandy said.

"What do we have to stop for?" I said.

"The tuna-fish sandwich," Sandy said.

When we got to the Broncos' hotel, the coaches and players were having lunch together in a ballroom with a long buffet table. Ham, turkey, roast beef, salami, cheese, you name it. Everything was there. Everything except tuna-fish salad. But say this for Sandy, he didn't choke.

"I really need a favor," he said to one of the hotel people. "I need a tuna-fish sandwich. To go."

The hotel guy disappeared through the kitchen doors.
Two minutes later he was back, with a tuna-fish sandwich
wrapped to go. Sandy thanked him, took the sandwich,
and hurried out for our trip up to the Giants' hotel. When
we walked into Bill Parcells's room, Sandy handed him
the tuna-fish sandwich.

"Thanks," Bill said.

The next day, the Giants celebrated their Super Bowl
victory by dousing Bill with Gatorade twice. And a few
days later Bill got around to looking at the films, like every
NFL coach does after every game, like I did when I was
the Raiders' coach. But as an analyst, I've never looked at
a tape of any of my games. My theory is that if I didn't like
something I said, I wouldn't know what to do about it the
next time, so I don't watch. I'm like the actor—I forget his
name—that I once saw on the Johnny Carson show.

"I don't watch any of my movies," I remember him
saying. "If you're an actor, you've got to be natural. I don't
want to do anything that would prompt me to act unnatu-
rally."

I'm the same way. If I heard myself say something I
didn't like, or saw myself do something I didn't like, I'd be
tempted not to do it the next time. But if I *did* change it,
then I wouldn't be reacting naturally, I'd be a phoney. All
I've ever tried to do on television is just be me. Usually
that means doing my Chalkboard and telling people sto-
ries about the players and the coaches. But every once in
a while, CBS has me do something that won't let me be
me, like the pool shoot I did in Atlantic City a few years
ago. Steve Mizerak, a real pro, was doing some trick shots
that gave our producer, Ed Goren, an idea.

"Let's set up a shot for John," Ed said. "You can shoot it, Steve, but we'll make it look like John did it."

"No, no," Steve said. "John can make the shot. I'll set up five balls, but John can make the shot."

As a teenager in the Daly City pool hall, I was a decent pool player. Of the good players there, I ranked somewhere from sixth to tenth, depending on how I was playing. It was an old pool hall on the second floor above a store. It had eight pool tables, three snooker tables, and five pinball machines. But now I was chalking my cue at a pool table in Atlantic City with television cameras on me.

"John knows how to handle a stick," Steve said. "I'll just set up the balls."

Steve placed five balls at various positions around the table, then he spotted the white cue ball.

"If you hit the red ball straight on," Steve told me, "every ball should fall."

I surveyed the table, leaned over, lined up my cue with the cue ball, and waited for Ed Goren to let me know when he was ready.

"Anytime, John," he said. "Anytime."

Steve Mizerak couldn't have stroked it any better. Click, clunk, the cue ball hit the red ball straight on. And then there were clunks all over the table. One by one, the five balls were on their way to different pockets. Schlump, schlump, schlump, schlump, schlump. All five balls disappeared. I looked up, searching for Ed Goren's face over near the cameras.

"That was just a rehearsal, John, the camera wasn't on," he said. "Can you do it again, please?"

Do it again? I'd never done that shot before in my life and now he wanted me to do it again! Steve lined up the balls again, I leaned over again, click went the cue ball again. But the cue ball hit the red ball slightly off-center, just enough to throw the angles off.

"Don't worry about it," I heard Ed say. "Let's keep trying it until we get it."

On the sixth try, all five balls thudded into five different pockets. When the show appeared on CBS, that was the only shot they had me taking. I wish they had shown all the misses. That would've been more like me.

JUST A BUNCH
OF GUYS

It started out as a fun thing, but now some people are taking my All-Madden teams seriously. Maybe too seriously.

Some players tell me it's in their contract that they get a bonus if they're on the All-Madden team. Some players even get annoyed if they're not on it. When the Giants were on their chartered jet going to Super Bowl XXI, they picked up CBS Sports Sunday, where I announced the 1986 team. I had a few Giants on it—Phil Simms, Joe Morris, Mark Bavaro, Brad Benson, Lawrence Taylor, Jim Burt, Carl Banks, Harry Carson, Phil McConkey. I even had an ex-Giant, Pat Summerall, as my place kicker. But no punter.

"What we're going to do is go for it," I joked, meaning go for either a first down or a field goal. "The fans love it when you go for it."

Early that Super Bowl week, Pat and I stopped by the Giants' hotel. As soon as we walked in, their All-Pro punter that season, Sean Landeta, glared at me.

"You're going to go for it every time, huh?" Sean said.

When we went over to the Denver Broncos' hotel, their place kicker, Rich Karlis, approached Pat.

"I respect you," Rich said, "but *I* should've been on the All-Madden team. At least with honorable mention."

I'm glad they take it seriously, because when I'm selecting the players each year, I take it seriously. But hey, guys, don't take it *too* seriously. That's not the idea. And the idea wasn't even my idea. It was John Robinson's idea. Long before he was the Los Angeles Rams' coach, John and I grew up together in Daly City, and like me, he's one of those guys who's always saying, "You know what you oughta do?" With us, it's not a suggestion. It's an order.

"You know what you oughta do?" John said to me during the 1985 season. "You oughta pick an all-NFL team with your kind of guys on it. Not an All-Pro team, just your kind of guys."

I liked it, and when I mentioned it to Terry O'Neil, then our executive producer at CBS, he liked it. "We'll do it," he said. "We'll put it on the Sunday between the conference championship games and the Super Bowl game." The only problem was, I forgot about it, until I happened to look at a promo on the monitor during a timeout in an NFC playoff game—in two weeks I'd be naming the first annual All-Madden team.

Oh, no, I thought, *I haven't even picked it.*

I wasn't worried. My producer would be Mike Arnold, who's on the same weird wavelength I'm on. What I didn't know was that Mike got switched to working on something else. Dave Blatt got the show, but then Dave couldn't do it either. By then the whole idea had been lost in the transition from one producer to another. I was home in California when I went over to San Francisco to view the segment that was scheduled to go on the next day. I couldn't believe it.

"Who cut this thing?" I roared. "We've got a shot of Jack Youngblood playing on artificial turf. His uniform's completely white, completely clean. No blood on it. Jack Youngblood's uniform always has some blood on it."

This team wasn't just another All-Pro team. This had to be different. This was the first annual All-Madden team. But the way it looked, this would be the last annual All-Madden team. There was only one thing I could do, and that was *not* to do the show, at least not with the segment that I had just seen. By that time, Mike Arnold had completed his other assignment and he was out in San Francisco, working on the Super Bowl XIX preview that CBS had shown that Saturday.

"I'm not doing this the way it is," I told Mike. "Call Terry O'Neil and tell him I'm not doing it."

I'd never done anything like that before at CBS, but I knew that this segment wasn't All-Madden, it was just another All-Highlights show.

"I know what you want," Mike said. "I brought some tapes of all the players you wanted, just in case. I'll put together a new show."

Mike stayed up all night reworking it, taking out the dull tapes and putting in the tapes that showed why these players were on the All-Madden team. I had *seen* them play that season, not just read or heard about them. And they were different. They were all good players. Some were even great players. But they were usually a little *different. My* kind of different. Like the 49ers' linebacker, Jack (Hacksaw) Reynolds, who once sawed an old car in half with a hacksaw when he was at the University of Tennessee because he was so pissed off at losing a game. Hacksaw was a natural for that first All-Madden team.

But every year I always put in a disclaimer. The only players considered for the All-Madden team each year are players in the games I work for CBS that season. If I didn't see a player from our CBS booth, I don't pick him. I'm not about to take somebody else's word on a guy, or go with what I've read in the papers. Since I have to see a guy play, and since I usually work games involving NFC teams, the All-Madden team has always been loaded with players on NFC teams. Nothing against the AFC players or the AFC teams, but if I don't happen to work their games, I don't pick them.

"This team doesn't make a lot of sense," I explained at the opening of our first All-Madden show after the 1984 season. "They have All-America teams, All-Pro teams, Pro Bowl teams, and those all make sense. This doesn't. This is just a bunch of guys that we've seen, that we've met, that we've watched play, that we've admired. I thought it would be kind of fun to just put 'em all together."

Pat Summerall and I discuss the selections each year over game action, close-up sideline shots, and taped comments from some of the players. During the show after the 1986 season, Lawrence Taylor, the Giants' linebacker, talked about how being chosen for the All-Madden team was "almost as good as getting a Super Bowl ring, but I want to know: what's his criteria for that team in the first place?"

Criteria?

"We don't talk qualifications, criteria, mayonnaise, we don't know those big words," I said to Pat that day. "We talk guys. You know, guys out there looking around to see what's going on. Just a bunch of guys we put together. If you and I were coaching, it'd be fun to coach these guys. If you or I were one of the players, it'd be fun to play with these guys."

Fun to get your uniform dirty with these guys. Joe Jacoby, the Redskins' 305-pound offensive tackle, caught the spirit of the team its first year.

"Seeing the mud on the jersey, the guy's shirttail hanging out, the mud in his face," Joe said. "I think the guys that John picked play that way."

Especially the offensive linemen. To me, they are the heart of a football team. In explaining why Tom Newberry, a guard for the Rams, was on the 1987 team, I said, "He holds the sweat well. He spits on himself." If you're a good offensive lineman, your uniform is going to get dirty and also a little bloody. No player has ever been bloodier week after week than Brad Benson, the Giants' offensive tackle on their Super Bowl XXI team. During that 1986 season, Brad had scar tissue on the bridge of his nose from getting rapped by the front of his helmet all those years. After the first or second play of each game, the bridge of his nose was bleeding. He always had a Band-Aid across it, but that didn't help much.

"I think I made this team basically because of my nose," Brad said. "I think I have the official nose of the John Madden team."

If it's my team, it's also got to be a little goofy. On the

1987 team I had four quarterbacks—Doug Williams of the Redskins, Wade Wilson of the Vikings, Joe Montana and Jim McMahon. "You can come out of the huddle," I suggested, "with four quarterbacks." Now that might confuse some football people, but Pat Summerall never blinked.

"That makes sense to me," Pat said. "I've been with you a long time."

On the 1986 team I had three centers—Jay Hilgenberg of the Bears, Billy Bryan of the Broncos, and Jeff Van Note of the Falcons. Jay Hilgenberg has been my kind of guy ever since he said, "What I like about football is that you don't have to take a shower before you go to work." Billy Bryan has so much tape on, he seems to be impersonating a mummy.

"If we ever need some tape," I told Pat Summerall, "we'll just pull a hunk off Bryan."

Jeff Van Note, the NFL's grand old man, was retiring after eighteen seasons, so we put together some before and after pictures. "This is what he looked like when he started—dark-haired guy, smooth cheeks," I said. "After about six or seven years, the scars started to come, down the forehead, into the nose. A little later, graying hair, receding, no teeth. That's an All-Madden type of player. Eighteen years in the pits. Did you ever wonder how many snaps he made in those eighteen years?" And speaking through his bushy beard, Jeff said he knew it was time to begin the rest of his life.

"I came into this league, my hair was jet black, now it's gray," he said. "After eighteen years in the trenches, in the pits, it's just time to get out of football. I need to get into something serious, another career. Maybe pro wrestling."

With three centers on the team, Pat Summerall had a

good question: how do you line up three centers on your offensive unit? Hey, that's why it's the All-Madden team, that's why it's different. Any team can have a center and two guards and two tackles and a tight end hunkered down. We're going to line up our three centers side by side.

"If the quarterback comes out of the huddle, he can go to any of these guys," I said. "If he gets a little woozy, a little delirious, if he doesn't know where he is, he can just wander out, go up to the line, and he'll always hit a center."

I didn't dare mention that for this to work we'd need three footballs as well as three centers. Hey, this is my team. If we have three centers up there on the line, we can have three footballs. But only one ball would be snapped.

"Now defensively, the nose tackle lines up on the center," I said. "But with three centers, where does he line up? The nose tackle won't know where to line up. And all those other defensive guys, they'll be walking around like question marks. When the quarterback comes up, he gets the ball and we go right on through. We trick 'em. With centers."

The year before, we tricked the offense with an All-Madden team that had seven nose tackles. Those guys are always in the middle of everything. I think they have the most fun.

I took Jim Burt of the Giants, Michael Carter of the 49ers, Dan Hampton of the Bears, Joe Klecko of the Jets, Howie Long of the Raiders, Leonard Marshall of the Giants, and Steve McMichael of the Bears, and lined them up together. No, not across the field. One behind the other.

Hey, if it's my team, it's also my defensive alignment. In the NFL, a nose tackle is always double-teamed, sometimes triple-teamed. He gets blocked by the center, then a guard comes over and hits him, sometimes the blocking back gets a piece of him. But with my seven nose tackles lined up one behind the other, the blockers wouldn't know where they were coming from. At the snap, my seven nose tackles would just run wild.

"We don't even call this a forty-three defense or a thirty-four or a forty-six or any of those numbers," I explained. "It's just the BGD: Big Guy Defense."

But as much as I love those big guys, I think that as a group, linebackers are the NFL's best players. They come to the game with fire in their eyes. If I ever had to go anyplace where I thought I might need some bodyguards, I'd take linebackers with me.

The best linebackers always have that wild look. Dick Butkus had that look when he was a Hall of Fame linebacker for the Bears, chomping at the bit, ready to go. Mike Singletary has that look now. Off the field, Mike is the sweetest guy you'd ever want to meet. But on the field, when he's staring through the facemask on his Bear helmet, you don't want to get in his way. Lawrence Taylor has that look. At his best, Lawrence is the NFL's most dominant player. He can drop back and cover on passes. He can sack the quarterback. If you run at him, he tackles you. If you run away from him, he runs all the way across the field and tackles you. Even in repose, he throws words like "criteria" at you. He's been All-Madden three of the four years, but I left him off the 1985 team. That was the season, he acknowledged later, when he was mixed up with cocaine.

Sometimes a player is so good that people don't realize

when he's *not* so good. That season I was one of the first to mention that L.T. wasn't playing well, or at least not at his usual level of excellence. He didn't dip down enough to be a bad player. He just slipped a small degree. But that small degree had made L.T. the best.

During the 1986 season, L.T. was as good as ever. Maybe better than ever. After he found out he had been selected for the 1986 All-Madden team, he spotted me in the Giants' locker room. "Your All-Madden team," he said, "that's the one where you had The Refrigerator as a wide receiver last year?" I nodded and said, "Yeah, that's the one." He just said, "Yeah, OK." He didn't ask, "How come I wasn't on it last year?" But now I knew he had seen it. And now I thought that maybe L.T. had brought up The Refrigerator, William Perry of the Bears, to let me know that he knew why he hadn't been on that All-Madden team. Deep down, he must have known why.

As for The Refrigerator being a wide receiver on the 1985 team, that was the year of The Refrigerator, a rookie defensive tackle whose weight depends on how long it's been since his last meal. Or his last snack.

Mike Ditka, the Bears' coach, wants The Fridge somewhere just over three hundred pounds. But his Bear teammates know it's not that easy for The Fridge to push himself away from the table. No matter what the big Toledo scale in Halas Hall reads when The Fridge steps on it, Dan Hampton might have the best scouting report on The Fridge's weight.

"William," says Dan, "is just a biscuit away from three-fifty."

But no matter what The Fridge weighed in 1985, he was the talk of the NFL—a defensive tackle who was also used in goal-line situations as a fullback. Including the

Bears' victory in Super Bowl XX, he carried the ball six times for a total of eight yards and three touchdowns. He also caught a pass for four yards and another touchdown. And that was the *only* pass thrown to him all season. One for one and a touchdown.

"When I want a wide receiver," I said over a tape of The Fridge catching that touchdown pass, "I want a *wide* receiver."

The Fridge and Jim McMahon helped to put the fun back in football. McMahon was my quarterback on that 1985 All-Madden team, but he was also a wide receiver. In addition to all those touchdown passes he threw, he also caught a touchdown pass. He and The Fridge were the perfect wide receivers for an All-Madden team—two guys who scored a touchdown every time they caught a pass. But as a quarterback, McMahon has endeared himself to me. I've never met a great quarterback who was normal, and McMahon is no exception. Anybody can slap hands or shake hands, but he celebrates a touchdown by head-butting his teammates.

Jim McMahon supplies what I call "good goofy," a spirit that every team needs.

Not that everybody on an All-Madden team has to be different. Some guys belong simply because they are so good at what they do. Walter Payton is the NFL's career rushing leader. But he was on three All-Madden teams for the other things he did for the Bears, like blocking and catching passes, sometimes even throwing passes. And if you think he knew how to destroy opposing defenses, listen to how he destroyed me.

"John who?" he said, upon learning he'd been named to the first All-Madden team. "Oh, that crazy guy who always talks with his hands."

Then there are the special-team guys, who really *are* different, like Phil McConkey, the Giants' wide receiver and punt returner. McConkey made my 1985 team not because of the way he caught passes or returned punts. Anyone can do that. He made the team because he had the guts to get into a fight in the middle of the Packers' bench area. Most players will tiptoe away from another team's bench, but McConkey started swinging at everybody in sight.

"We have a lot of fighters on this team," I explained, "but we need a fight starter, and that's McConkey, five feet nine and fighting the other team's bench."

McConkey likes to hit people, but in 1986 he made the All-Madden team because he's the kind of guy who likes to *get* hit. On one punt return, I thought a tackler had cut him in two. Most guys would get up counting their fingers. He bounced up waving his arms; he couldn't wait to get hit that hard again. He also made it as a team-leader-outer. When the Giants ran onto the field before a game at Giants Stadium, he was the first one out, waving a towel to stir up the fans.

"In the navy, he was a helicopter *pilot,*" I said over a clip of him waving a white towel over his head. "Now he thinks he's a *helicopter.*"

Sometimes a player's name is enough to get him on the All-Madden team, like Paul Butcher of the Lions' special teams.

"What a great name for a cover guy," I said as he tackled a kickoff returner. "Hey coach, who's your cover guy? *Butcher.*"

Sometimes a player receives honorable mention for what he does off the field. Back when I was riding trains, Bill Bain, the Rams' offensive tackle, took a train from his home to the Amtrak stop near the Rams complex. I had to pick him. Bain on the train. When the Giants swept through Super Bowl XXI with twelve consecutive victories, Harry Carson was the designated dumper of Gatorade on Coach Bill Parcells near the end of every game. Harry would carry the orange bucket in one hand as he sneaked around behind some other players, switch it to the other hand and splash, do the dumpski on the coach. Definitely honorable mention.

"It's a big honor to be on John's team," Gary Fencik, the Bears' safety, said on our show after the 1986 season. "I've made a lot of different teams, but believe it or not, this is one of the few teams where you actually get a gift when you make it."

I'm real proud of the gift. The first two years, each member of the All-Madden team got a print of a François Cloutier oil painting showing a football player standing on the sideline in the rain. His uniform is dirty, his cleats are muddy. He's got a long coat draped over his shoulders, but he's holding his helmet in his right hand, ignoring the rain. My kind of football player. The poster was beautiful, but then Bob Stenner, our CBS producer, came up with a better idea.

"You know Ed White, the guard for the Chargers and the Vikings? Now he's a sculptor," Bob said. "Why don't you get him to do a statue that will be the All-Madden gift?"

Ed White had been my kind of football player. He suffered in the snow with the Vikings and he sweated in the heat with the Chargers, but no matter what the weather was like, he was a big eater. When he went to a restaurant, he didn't look at the menu, he ordered it. If there had been an All-Madden team years ago, Ed would've been on it. And now I decided that he should be the All-Madden sculptor.

"Do one in bronze," I said.

It's beautiful. I think it's the nicest football trophy I've ever seen, nicer than the Heisman Trophy because it's not that stylish. It looks like it was molded out of mud instead of bronze, and that's the way the All-Madden statue should look. Each member of the All-Madden team now receives a bas-relief replica of the original sculpture that we displayed on our show after the 1986 season. When the show was over, I had a question.

"Where does this statue go now?"

"Back to the CBS building in New York," somebody said. "They want to put it up on the thirtieth floor."

"This trophy doesn't belong on the thirtieth floor," I said. "It belongs in my house. Ship it to my house."

And that's where it is, up on a shelf, near the bar off my family room. And that's where it stays.

MY NUMBERS GAME

umbers have always fascinated me—not the numbers of mathematics, but the numbers themselves. The numbers that football and baseball players wear. And the numbers that famous people, if they wore sports uniforms, would wear. Men and women. To me, Ronald Reagan would be wearing 16, Bill Cosby 12, Elizabeth Taylor 32, Paul Newman 22, Katharine Hepburn 18 and Pope John Paul II 73.

I've always felt that you can put a number on a person that tells about that person. Certain numbers have certain characteristics. It's not always something you can explain.

There's no rhyme or reason for it. But when you see a certain person in a certain number, you know it's the perfect number. In football, O. J. Simpson was a perfect 32, but so was Jack Tatum, the Raiders' free safety, who was one of the NFL's hardest hitters. To me, 32 is a skills number, but it also fits people with some hardness. Elizabeth Taylor and Muhammad Ali are both a perfect 32.

Ronald Reagan, Johnny Carson, and Bob Hope are each a 16, a number with a certain softness about it. Nancy Reagan is also a 16; just wrap her and the president in a 16 package. Katharine Hepburn is an 18, not quite so well known as a 16, but a little classier, someone who's not out in front all the time. Paul Newman is a 22, always a speed number.

To wear 12, you need to be a leader with charisma. Some of the NFL's best quarterbacks have worn 12—Joe Namath (the best quarterback I've ever seen), Roger Staubach, Ken Stabler. Bill Cosby and Jack Nicklaus each would be a 12, but somebody like Joe Frazier is a 51, a linebacker's number, Dick Butkus's number when he was a Bears linebacker. Joe reminds me of a guy who would stand there and plug something. He'd be perfect in a Bears uniform. These numbers go back to when my pal John Robinson and I were kids. We never played football or baseball or anything else without being someone, and we'd never be someone without being a number.

"I'm seventy-four," I used to say.

I was a big kid, and Bob Toneff, a big defensive tackle for the 49ers, wore 74. In those years you couldn't buy a 49er jersey, like you can now. I just crayoned 74 in red on my white sweatshirt. Nobody had their name on their jersey then, just their number. So the number was more important than the player's name. I still think of myself as a 74.

You can have good players with good numbers. Or bad players with bad numbers. Or some players who would be better if they wore better numbers.

Back when I was the Raiders' coach, and even before that, as the Hancock Junior College coach, I assigned numbers to all my players. I'm sure I'm the only coach in football history who ever assigned numbers.

Of all the Raider numbers, I'm proudest of two—Art Shell's 78, and Dave Casper's 87. Art Shell was a huge offensive tackle, six feet five and more than three hundred pounds. He filled out a 78 perfectly. Dave Casper was six four and 230, not quite tall enough to be an 89, but a perfect 87. Our little wide receiver, Cliff Branch, had been a world-class sprinter at the University of Colorado. I assigned him 31, a good number. But if I had it to do over again, he'd have been 22. To me, 22 means a bullet.

Some numbers are angular. To wear an 8 or a 9, you have to be really tall. James Stewart and Pat Summerall are both an 88. If you're short, 2 is a good number. Woody Allen is a 2, a little place kicker. But if you're little and a great athlete, you're a 1, like Bill Shoemaker, a perfect 1.

Numbers for football players and baseball players are necessary for the fans, but I never thought basketball numbers made any sense. At a basketball game, you see a player's whole body. After the first look, you don't need to know his number. Maybe that's why football and baseball numbers identify so well with an athlete. You need his number to know who's under that helmet or cap.

In the following lists, I've assigned numbers to entertainment personalities, politicians, businessmen, and sportspeople who usually don't wear numbers. One by one, as the names were thrown at me, I pictured the person and pictured the number. If some of your favorite people in these categories aren't on the lists, it's probably because I don't know them well enough to picture them.

ENTERTAINMENT:

Woody Allen	2
Fred Astaire	3
Lauren Bacall	19
Jack Benny	9
Milton Berle	17
Humphrey Bogart	7
Marlon Brando	52
George Burns	2
Jimmy Cagney	32
Johnny Carson	16
Johnny Cash	77
Gary Cooper	24
Bill Cosby	12
Bing Crosby	16
Bette Davis	12
Sammy Davis, Jr.	24
John Denver	10

Neil Diamond	22
Phil Donahue	8
Kirk Douglas	19
Clint Eastwood	22
Peter Falk	6
Jane Fonda	6
Henry Fonda	17
Michael J. Fox	2
Clark Gable	19
James Garner	28
Cary Grant	22
Gene Hackman	81
Merle Haggard	18
Larry Hagman	16
Katharine Hepburn	18
Charlton Heston	88
Dustin Hoffman	2
Bob Hope	16
Michael Jackson	12
Burt Lancaster	5
David Letterman	81

Jack Lemmon	24
Jerry Lewis	28
Barbara Mandrell	26
Dean Martin	12
Steve Martin	17
Mary Tyler Moore	17
Marilyn Monroe	32
Eddie Murphy	12
Willie Nelson	32
Bob Newhart	4
Paul Newman	22
Jack Nicholson	12
Carrol O'Connor	26
Dolly Parton	76
Joe Piscopo	64
Elvis Presley	76
Don Rickles	6
Joan Rivers	11
Edward G. Robinson	52
Kenny Rogers	17
Diana Ross	6

Arnold
    Schwarzenegger   72

Tom Selleck   18

Paul Simon   3

Frank Sinatra   16

James Stewart   88

Elizabeth Taylor   32

John Wayne   72

Vanna White   11

Bruce Willis   9

Flip Wilson   9

Oprah Winfrey   72

POLITICS, BUSINESS:

Jimmy Carter   11

Dwight D.
    Eisenhower   55

Gerald Ford   72

Howard Hughes   89

Lee Iacocca   77

Rev. Jesse Jackson   24

Lyndon B. Johnson   23

John F. Kennedy	26
Abraham Lincoln	12
Richard Nixon	16
Jacqueline Onassis	19
Tip O'Neill	75
Pope John Paul II	73
Nancy Reagan	16
Ronald Reagan	16
Franklin D. Roosevelt	74
Harry S. Truman	55
Donald Trump	32
Ted Turner	11
George Washington	72

SPORTS:

Muhammad Ali	32
George Allen	12
Arthur Ashe	9
Red Auerbach	3
Seve Ballesteros	63
Paul Brown	24

Jimmy Connors	5
Angel Cordero, Jr.	3
Howard Cosell	19
Al Davis	32
Jack Dempsey	72
Mike Ditka	82
Angelo Dundee	3
Chris Evert	32
Weeb Ewbank	51
Charles O. Finley	30
George Foreman	74
Joe Frazier	51
Joe Gibbs	61
Pancho Gonzalez	6
Steffi Graf	19
Marvelous Marvin Hagler	22
Ben Hogan	12
Larry Holmes	78
Bruce Jenner	88
K. C. Jones	33
Bobby Knight	83
Tom Landry	88

Ivan Lendl	16
Sugar Ray Leonard	16
Carl Lewis	26
Sonny Liston	55
Vince Lombardi	72
Nancy Lopez	36
Joe Louis	36
John McEnroe	3
Rocky Marciano	23
Edwin Moses	36
Brent Musberger	5
Martina Navratilova	19
Byron Nelson	74
Jack Nicklaus	12
Chuck Noll	61
Greg Norman	19
Jesse Owens	22
Arnold Palmer	9
Bill Parcells	63
Floyd Patterson	82
Pat Riley	17

Sugar Ray Robinson	32
Pete Rozelle	7
Vin Scully	6
Bill Shoemaker	1
Don Shula	36
Sam Snead	16
Jimmy (The Greek) Snyder	95
Michael Spinks	99
Mark Spitz	28
George Steinbrenner	17
Dick Stockton	19
Hank Stram	5
Pat Summerall	88
Jim Thorpe	32
Gene Tunney	88
Mike Tyson	72
Peter Ueberroth	18
Bill Walsh	19
Tom Watson	19
John Wooden	12

"I'M BO DEREK"

hen it happened, I wasn't even aware of it. I had settled into my seat for the Hagler–Leonard middleweight championship fight at Caesars Palace in Las Vegas on April 6, 1987, and the ring announcer was introducing the "celebrities" at ringside, one by one. At fights, beautiful actresses always get a big hand. And when Bo Derek was introduced, the crowd responded with a roar. Joan Collins also got a big welcome. So did the Reverend Jesse Jackson, Frank Sinatra, Don Rickles, Telly Savalas, Gene Hackman, and Chevy Chase. In between, I was introduced. I stood up, waved quickly and sat down. I heard applause, but I wasn't measuring it. After a few more introductions, it was time for the fight.

"You got the biggest hand," somebody said to me. "Bigger than Bo Derek."

I was too impatient for the fight to start to think much about it then. But after Leonard won a split decision, I was walking down the stairs toward the Caesars Palace swimming pool when my son, Mike, noticed Bo Derek up ahead of us in her black homburg and black sweater.

"She's really beautiful," Mike said.

I had to agree. Then I realized she was walking toward us. But when Bo Derek is walking toward you, you don't think she's walking toward *you*. You see her looking at you, but you think she's really looking over your shoulder at someone behind you. The next thing I knew, she spoke to me.

"Excuse me, John," she said. "I'm Bo Derek, and I just wanted to say hello."

All those guys I grew up with in Daly City would never believe Bo Derek introducing herself to *me*. But unlike some actresses, she hadn't been sitting at ringside to be seen. She and her husband John have been going to the big fights in Vegas for several years. We talked about how Sugar Ray Leonard had been able to win after a virtual five-year layoff, then we went our separate ways. Mike and I had something to eat, then we went up to our room. But almost everybody I saw that night and the next day kept mentioning to me that of all the people who had been introduced, I got the biggest hand.

I'm not going to con you. Getting a big hand at a big fight was nice, and I appreciated it, but if I'd received the smallest hand, that would've been all right too. I just don't think of myself as a celebrity, but if other people do, I guess I am.

Anyway, after the fight, I stayed over in Vegas because

Virginia was coming in. She doesn't particularly like fights, but she likes Vegas, so she preferred to come over for a few days after the fight. Mike left to finish his senior year at Harvard, and Virginia hadn't arrived yet, so the night after the fight I went down to the Caesars Palace coffee shop for dinner. I ordered Chinese food, and was reading a newspaper when I noticed Bo Derek, her husband, and two other people sit down a few tables away. The next thing I knew, one of their friends walked over to where I was sitting.

"Mr. Madden," he said, pointing to their table, "Bo and John would like you to join them."

The problem was, I had already ordered. I didn't want to go over to their table and eat in front of them while they were still waiting for their food to come.

"Thank you," I said, "I'll be over in a few minutes."

After I finished my dinner, I sat with them and we talked mostly about the fight, then I went up to my room, watched television for a while, and went to sleep. When I mentioned all this to Gene Nelson on his KSFO radio show the next morning, he had the best line.

"You're the only guy I know," Gene told me, "who would put food ahead of Bo Derek."

Like I say, I don't think of myself as a celebrity. I went to the Hagler–Leonard fight to do a spot for CBS, to hang out in Vegas for a few days, and to see the fight. I didn't go there to be introduced. But through a combination of circumstances, I've come to realize that people know me. Some know me as the Raiders' former coach. Others know me from my television and radio commercials. Some from the NFL games I do, others from my books, some from the RKO radio spots I used to do, as well as the KSFO spots I still do.

Add it all up, and a lot of people know me. But if somebody had tried to plan all this, it never would have worked. Quit coaching, do some goofy commercials, do some NFL games with a chalkboard, do the books, and *presto,* you'll be a celebrity. Maybe that's why it did work. Because it wasn't planned.

It's a little like how if you need a loan, the bank won't let you in the door. But if you're rich, the bank will send a limo for you. Some people try desperately to be famous, but it never happens. Others don't even try and it happens. But just because people know you, it doesn't necessarily mean that they like you. During my son Mike's freshman year at Harvard, he and several other students were watching an NFL game I was doing. Among the students was a young lady who was obviously not impressed with what I was saying or what I was doing with my chalkboard.

"Out of the blue," Mike told me later, "she says, 'Don't you think this John Madden is weird?'

"People are always saying that, kidding me, so I play it off," Mike said. "But then she says, 'Don't you really think he's *weird?*' And then it hits me, she doesn't realize that's my dad she's talking about. I go, 'Well, no, I think he's pretty good. He's informative; he won an Emmy last year.' But she says, 'I know, everybody thinks he's good and everybody likes him, but I just think he's weird. I've had enough of him. He's weird.'

"I go, 'Well, Patty, you happen to be talking about my father,' and she says, 'What?' I say, 'That's my dad.' She turns and says, 'Nick, what's Mike's last name?' Nick tells her, 'Madden.'

"Now she turns to me and says, 'Your last name is Madden?' I tell her, 'I told you, he's my dad.' Now she turns to Nick again and says, 'Is John Madden really Mike's dad?' and Nick says, 'That's him on TV.' Now she turns to me and says, 'Oh, I'm *so* sorry.' "

Patty didn't have to apologize. I *am* weird. But maybe that weirdness helps me from taking myself too seriously. Maybe that helps me cope with fame.

When you start to believe you're a celebrity, that's when you can get into trouble. That's when you start to act like somebody you're not. Whenever I'm invited to one of those "celebrity" things, I try to avoid it if I can. Especially if it's a cocktail party. Some people know how to hold a drink and munch an hors d'oeuvre and when they're introduced to somebody, still be able to shake hands. The few times I've gone to one of those deals, by the time I get a drink and get something to eat, I've run out of hands. If I'm introduced to somebody and try to shake hands, I either spill the drink or drop the hors d'oeuvre.

I know some people who would kill to get an invitation to one of those parties. But if I had my choice, I'd rather sit outside on a park bench and watch the real celebrities drive up for the party.

About the only cocktail party Virginia and I go to is the one CBS has every year in Los Angeles for its affiliates. I even put on a suit and a tie. I really enjoy myself. I'm like most of the other people there, I like to gawk at guys I consider *real* celebrities—Larry Hagman, Bob Newhart, Tom Selleck.

When I met Larry Hagman, all I could think was, *Hey, you're J.R.,* but I didn't say that to him. I figured he gets that everywhere he goes. Besides, he just wanted to talk about pro football.

I found Bob Newhart to be a down-to-earth guy. Plus I

really respect him. He can get laughs without saying anything dirty. With me, he can get laughs just by picking up a telephone. Whatever he does, whatever he says, I crack up. I'm the same way when I see Eddie Murphy and Rodney Dangerfield. When Eddie laughs, I laugh. When Rodney twists his neck, I laugh.

I've gotten to know Rodney on the Miller Lite commercials. He likes to come in, do his lines and get out. No hanging around. No small talk. He's involved in what he's doing and he expects everybody else to be involved.

One time we were doing a radio commercial and he was sprawled in a chair, relaxing between takes. He had unbuttoned his shirt. He had even unbuttoned the top of his pants. But then he got involved in the wording of the dialogue in the script. To make his point, he jumped up to read the dialogue the way he wanted it. And his pants fell down.

No big deal. Rodney just kept doing the dialogue. When he finished, he pulled up his pants.

Being a celebrity is sometimes confining. I don't go to many baseball or basketball games anymore. It's hard to watch a game when you know other people are watching you. I stay home more now. Some people have wondered if I consider our new house at Blackhawk in Danville a symbol of success, but it has nothing to do with any symbols. All my life I'd wanted to live on a golf course or on an ocean. That probably goes back to when I was a caddie as a kid in Daly City, where I could walk to the ocean. Virginia and I had looked at homes in Palm Springs, but then we decided that we could only live there from January until May, when it just got too hot even to play golf. We also had thought about moving to Monterey, but decided to stay in Pleasanton, where we had lived ever since

1967, when I joined the Raiders as an assistant coach. Then one day Virginia had lunch at Blackhawk and decided to look at some houses there. When she got home, I was watching television.

"I just saw the most beautiful house in the world," she said.

"Yeah," I said, not taking my eyes off the TV screen. "Another beautiful house."

"You have to see this house," she said.

"Yeah," I said, still not looking up.

"C'mon, drive back with me and you can see for yourself."

"Nah," I said. "This house is fine."

"At least take a look at it with me."

I agreed. I figured I'd see something about it I didn't like and shoot it down and that would be it. Pick on something, anything. Tell her I hated it or that it just didn't appeal to me. But when I walked in, right away I liked the high ceilings. When you're six four, you like high ceilings. I kept walking through the house, looking for something I hated, something that didn't appeal to me. The next thing I knew, I'd walked through the whole house without finding something I hated. I hadn't been able to shoot it down.

"Yeah," I said, "it's really a nice house."

I think Virginia knew I loved it as much as she did. We looked at it again a few days later, and decided to buy it. If she hadn't found it, I would've been happy staying in the Pleasanton house, which I use as an office now. But this big place at Blackhawk really turned out to be a dream house. Not just the house, but also the surroundings. With the ninth tee of the Falls course just behind my garage, I can go out and play nine holes early in the morning or late in the afternoon. I can take a quick swim in my backyard pool in the morning.

This house lets me be active, but not too active. Virginia knows better than to expect me to do the gardening or be handy around the house. I don't even mow the lawn.

When we were first married, we lived in Santa Maria, California, in a little house with a little lawn in front and a little backyard. One day I was mowing in the backyard, keeping my eye on the grass. I walked into the T-shaped metal clothesline. Split my head open above the eye, bled all over. That's the last time I mowed the lawn.

"You did it on purpose," Virginia has said ever since. "I know you did it on purpose."

Around the house, I'm a mechanical moron. I just know that if I tried to put in a light switch, I'd blow the house up. I don't paint or put up wallpaper. I've got arthritis in my right shoulder from playing football, and it hurts too much for me to paint and put up wallpaper.

Virginia also knows that I'm not a social butterfly at the country club. If anything, I'm a social elephant.

I like to go to the men's grill in the Blackhawk club-house for lunch. But that's not going to a country club. That's like going to a good coffee shop with the guys. To me, a country club means getting dressed up to go to the dance on Saturday night. No, thanks. I'm not the type to go to the dance on Saturday night, just like I'm not the type to go on the Johnny Carson show. Hey, I watch Johnny Carson just about every night he's on. I think he's super, and I've been asked to be on his show. But it's like those celebrity cocktail parties where I'd rather sit outside and watch the real celebrities drive up. With the Johnny Carson show, I'd rather sit home and watch it. I'm a fan, and I wouldn't want to spoil that feeling for the show that I have as a fan.

To be honest, there's another reason why I don't want to go on the Johnny Carson show. The real reason is, I could never see myself coming out through that curtain, then walking over to the chair next to Johnny Carson's desk. I wouldn't know what to do after I came out through that curtain. Everybody else seems to be so natural. They come out through that curtain, they bow and wave, then they go over to Johnny Carson and shake hands or kiss. Not me. I'd probably trip and fall.

I guess I just don't know how to be a celebrity. And if I ever start to take myself too seriously as a celebrity, all I have to do is buy the papers at the newsstand down the block from my New York apartment.

The newsdealer knows me. He knows me so well, he calls me "Bill." I think he's got me confused with Bill Madden, a sportswriter on the New York *Daily News.* I've never had the heart to tell him that he's got us mixed up. And besides, he's doing me a favor.

If that newsdealer calls me Bill, I know I can't be much of a celebrity.

RED FLARES
AND FARMERS

ow that I don't ride trains anymore, I miss the people I met in the club cars and the dining cars. Riding along an interstate highway now, sometimes I wonder if those people are on a train somewhere. I wonder especially about those who were on our train the night of the Sing Sing Prison break.

On the Tuesday before the Redskins were to play a Saturday game in Denver, late in the 1986 season, I hurried through Grand Central Terminal's big marble lobby. I had my ticket for the Lake Shore Limited that was scheduled to leave at 7:35 P.M. and get me to Chicago early the next afternoon. There I had a short layover before taking the California Zephyr, which would get me to Denver on Thursday morning, in plenty of time to visit the two teams. But as soon as I got to the gate at Grand Central, I found out I might miss my connection in Chicago.

"They're holding us up for an hour, maybe more," a conductor said. "There's a fire on the tracks up near Sing Sing."

When you ride Amtrak north out of Grand Central, up between the brick tenements of upper Manhattan, past Yankee Stadium, and through Westchester County along the east bank of the Hudson River, you come to Sing Sing's gray walls, with armed guards in the towers. The prison has more than two thousand inmates. It's one of America's most famous prisons, the "big house" in those old Hollywood movies. And when we got close to Sing Sing that night, there was smoke, but no fire. About an hour before we were to leave Grand Central, two murderers and a burglar had set off smoke bombs to distract prison guards. They had scaled a fence and used a rope made from shoelaces to drop down a forty-foot wall to the railroad tracks and escape into the darkness.

By now the tracks had been closed. Dozens of prison guards, state troopers, railroad police, and local police were carrying shotguns and rifles as they roamed the tracks, searching for the escapees.

We had left Grand Central about two hours late, then stopped and started a few times. Close to Sing Sing, we stopped again. I was in the club car when all our lights went out. Our entire train was without electricity. No lights. No heat. No power in our engine. The electrified third rail had been turned off so that the guards could look for the escapees without having to worry about being electrocuted. On this foggy, chilly night out of an Alfred Hitchcock movie, the only lights we could see were the eerie red flares that the guards had put along the tracks.

"Don't be afraid, John," I heard a man say with a nervous laugh, "we'll be out of the tunnel in a few seconds."

He was kidding me about the Miller Lite commercial, the one where I hide behind the counter of the club-car bar when the train goes through a tunnel. I laughed, but I felt edgy: we didn't know how many escapees were out there—three or twenty-three. By that time, I learned later, the burglar had been caught, but the two murderers weren't recaptured until the next evening. One was found hiding inside a sailboat in a driveway in a nearby town, the other in a parked car in another town. But no matter what the situation, there'll always be some people who think it's funny. To the tune of "Less filling, tastes great," some guys in the club car were singing:

"Yea, troopers . . . yea, prisoners."

On the commuter trains, people were allowed to get off and take buses or cabs to the towns north of the prison. But on the Lake Shore Limited we were stuck until the tracks reopened. To get our minds off the possibility of the escapees jumping on the train, one woman tried to get everybody in the club car to sing Christmas carols. Nobody was interested. Another woman offered tranquilizers. Another woman was afraid that if the escapees got on the train, they would attack her.

"I'm wiping my makeup off," she said. "I'll be so ugly, they won't even look at me."

By then, the air in the club car was stuffy. One of the men at the end of the car opened a door, but some people told him to close it.

"If the prisoners get on the train," I heard somebody say, "they'll walk right into this car."

To help keep the passengers calm, the woman bartender had turned on a flashlight and was handing out free drinks. But the delay had created another problem. The train's engineer and crew are allowed to work only so many hours. I don't know what time they had started work that day, but when it got close to midnight, their hours were up.

"The new crew was supposed to take over in Albany," one of the crew told me. "But we're still two hours away from Albany."

Technically, the train couldn't move until a new crew took over. Somebody had to check that Amtrak in Washington would allow the train to go to the next station with the old crew. Finally, after five hours of sitting there with the lights out, we got moving again. Overall, we were about seven hours late. I didn't get to Denver until Friday morning.

When I looked back on being in that dark train, I realized that I never had that closed-in claustrophobic feeling that I've had in airplanes or elevators. I was trapped in this hunk of metal in the middle of nowhere, but I didn't *feel* trapped.

Maybe it was the excitement of the adventure. Maybe it was just being on a train, an environment where I've been comfortable ever since I stopped traveling by plane. Maybe it was the club car's being a conversational hangout. That's what I miss most about trains—sitting with people, talking with them, learning from them. Especially people whose lives are so completely different from mine. Like farmers.

Of all the people I ever met on trains, I found farmers

to be the most interesting. On one level, farmers live a completely different life than I do, but in another sense their life isn't that much different.

On my first few train trips, I could never understand why anybody would be a farmer all their life. In our conversations, all they did was complain. Not enough rain, too much rain. Not enough sun, too much sun. Not enough cool weather, too much cool weather. Their life depended on the elements, and the elements were never perfect. One night, rolling through the Iowa cornfields, I finally asked a farmer why he was a farmer.

"Because I'm a farmer," he said. "That's what I do."

The more I thought about it, the more I realized that if every person was asked why they are what they are, just about everybody would have a similar answer. Like if somebody asked me why I'm a football analyst on television.

"I'm a football guy," I'd say. "Played football. Coached football. Talk about football on television. That's what I do."

Talking to farmers, I also realized why America works. Whenever our conversation got around to New York, farmers would say, "Muggers, they steal your money, they steal your car. You'd never get me to go to New York. No, sir, not me. I live in God's country." To farmers, their farmland is God's country. To city people, that farmland is the sticks. "I need the action," city people say. "I need big buildings, restaurants, theaters, discos." You need both types. If everybody wanted to live in God's country, pretty soon there'd be no room for the farms. If everybody wanted to live in the city, there'd be no farms. And without farms, we might get a little hungry.

Most farmers work seven days a week. Or they make

sure somebody else is doing the work if they can't. I once asked a Wisconsin dairy farmer if he ever went to Green Bay or Milwaukee to see the Packers.

"Nobody tells the cows that it's Sunday, nobody tells the cows that the Packers are playing," he said with a laugh. "Those cows have to be milked every day. No one tells the cows it's Christmas morning or New Year's morning or that today's my birthday. You got to take care of those cows every day."

Some farmers don't like to leave their farms. On a train to Seattle once I sat with a farmer who was traveling with his brother and his brother's wife. He told me he was fifty-five, a bachelor who did his farmwork every morning and played golf at his country club every afternoon. I had never associated a farmer with playing golf. He was a pretty good golfer too, an eight handicap as I remember. And he talked about how he had a satellite dish on his farm and every night he picked up baseball and basketball games from all over the country. But he had never been away from his farm before.

"They talked me into taking this trip," he told me, meaning his brother and sister-in-law. "But it's like I kidnapped myself. I never been off the farm before."

Whenever I saw him after that, he was worrying about whether everything was all right back on his farm. He was a fish out of water. But that's why I loved to talk to the farmers. They're different. I like different people, different places, different fun. On another trip to Seattle, a few years ago, I had the most fun I ever had on a train. Well, not exactly on a train, but it happened because I was on a train. When a freight train ahead of us derailed, we had to stop in Culbertson, Montana.

"We're going to be here awhile," the conductor said.

"You can walk around town if you want. We'll blow the whistle when we want you back."

On the dusty little main street, I walked into a saloon that was right out of a John Wayne movie and pounded a fist on the bar. "Set up the house," I said. "I'm buying!" The bartender stared at me, then he started pouring drinks for the half dozen townspeople sitting around.

"I've always wanted to do this," I said, laughing. "Set up the house."

In that little bar, a Miller Lite commercial had come to life. And no one enjoyed it more than I did. All the drinks for the next few hours couldn't have come to more than maybe twenty-five dollars, which I considered a bargain. When the train whistle blew, I left some money on the bar.

"One more time," I said. "Set up the house one more time."

If I ever get near Culbertson on my bus, I'll have to stop in that bar again.

NO BANJO ORDERS

Nobody enjoys good food more than I do, but I don't pretend to be a gourmet. I don't go to a restaurant for a dining experience. I go there to eat.

If I had my way, I'd rather belly up to a trough than sit around sipping cocktails and munching on carrot sticks for half an hour before the food arrives. As soon as I sit down, I like to start eating. That's why I seldom go to restaurants where you need a reservation, or where you need to get dressed up. If you need a reservation, it's too crowded. If you need to get dressed up, it's too fancy. Either way, the service will be too slow. Maybe not for most people, but for me it will be. If waiters or waitresses introduce themselves, the service is already too slow.

"My name is——," they'll say.

As soon as I hear that, I feel like saying that I didn't come here for a meaningful relationship. I really don't care what their name is. I'm hungry and I'm there to eat. I've never considered eating to be a social deal. To me, eating is just that. Eating. Enjoying your food. And not having to order a cocktail or two before you order your food.

"Would you like a cocktail?" they always ask.

It used to be, Would you like a *drink*? You used to have a drink and eat spaghetti. Now you have a cocktail and eat pasta. I guess it sounds more refined. I don't drink much hard liquor or wine. If you consider a Lite Beer a cocktail, I'll order one, but I won't let them walk away without taking the food order. I hate those drills where they bring you cocktails, but no food. The next thing you know, they're back asking if you want another cocktail. But before the waitress walks away with the food order, I add a reminder.

"No banjo orders, please."

Banjo orders, that's when they string out the orders as if they were strings on a banjo. Say someone at our table orders clams and someone else orders chicken soup and I order a salad. In some restaurants they'll bring the clams first. When the clams are finished, they'll bring the soup. When the soup is finished, they'll bring the salad.

"Bring 'em all at the same time," I say. "No banjo orders."

In most fancy restaurants now, you always get cocktailed and banjoed. That's one of the reasons I like Mexican restaurants. As soon as you sit down, you've got a bowl of chips and a bowl of salsa. You're eating right away. Growing up in northern California, I developed a taste for Mexican food. For my favorite meal now, I go to Cocina de Luís, which translates to Louie's kitchen, a Mexican restaurant in Dublin, California, not far from our Danville home. Like most of the good Mexican restaurants, it's a family operation. Louie Hermida is the cook, his wife Josie is the hostess. Their daughters Elaine, Wanda, Cecile and Jerri are the waitresses, and Louie Jr. and their granddaughter Lilliana also work there. And their food is the best. Louis grew up in Juárez, Mexico, where his parents had a restaurant. He has so much pride in what he does and he's so good at it that, even if you ask for something that's not on the menu, he'll make it. Like the chorizo (sausage) and beans that he's always nice enough to make for me.

After the chips and salsa, I usually order the Nachos a la Luís (topped with shrimp), chorizo and beans with flour tortillas, and the chile colorado, New Mexico (chunks of beef in a red chile sauce) with a Lite Beer or a Diet Pepsi, or two.

I like my Mexican food hot. I mean *hot.* But hot sauces come in different degrees of hot. Louie has mild, medium, and hot red and green chile sauces, a bell-pepper sauce, and a jalapeño-pepper sauce. Josie tells me that the best red chiles come from New Mexico, where she grew up in Albuquerque. To get the best red chiles, she has her sister Sophie send up a fresh supply from New Mexico twice a month. But unless you like a very hot chile sauce, be careful. When their restaurant opened, in 1979, Louie made a red sauce with chiles that Sophie had labeled "very hot." He and Josie loved it, and they put it on the menu.

"But the first few days," Josie says, "we realized that some people could not eat these very hot chiles. Their eyes were watering. Their noses were running. They were gasping for air. I went into the kitchen and told my husband that we had to either tone down our red chile sauce or call the fire department."

After that, Sophie sent the milder chiles. But the hottest item in Mexican food is *pepín*, little red peppers that Louie calls bee-bees. One night I took Dave Casper, the tight end on the Raiders back when I was the coach, to Cocina de Luís for a meal. Dave had told me he liked his Mexican food really hot, so I ordered *pepín*. When the red bee-bees arrived, Dave mixed a few in his burrito.

With his first bite, Dave's face turned as red as a beet. He broke out in a sweat. Then he turned as white as a sheet, like he had lost all his blood. But he survived. When your food is that hot, it doesn't do much good to drink a cold beer or a cold soda. The trick, I'm told, is to put sugar on your tongue.

After a good meal, that's when I like to sit around and talk, not before. That's what I like about one of my favorite New York places, the Café La Fortuna, a dark Italian coffee house with brick walls. I learned about it while reading a book on John Lennon, about how he hung out there because nobody bothered him. No matter who walks in, the people sipping espresso or cappucino at their little tables never even look up.

The best food in New York is pizza. You can't get really good pizza anywhere outside New York, just like you can't get really good Mexican food in New York. If a good New

York pizza place could trade locations with a good Mexican restaurant in California, they'd both get rich. But it's not that simple. I'm told that New York's good water helps to make the pizza dough better, just like the fresh California ingredients help to make the Mexican food there better.

But what I like about my favorite New York pizza place, T&R's on Columbus Avenue, goes beyond the pizza.

I'll be sitting there, munching a slice of pizza and reading the papers, when an old woman or an old man will wander in and order a slice. But when those old people try to pay, the guy behind the counter will wave them off. The guy behind the counter never makes a big deal out of it. Just a quick wave and a smile. I don't know for sure, but my guess is that most of these old people are homeless. Whenever I see them wander out with their slice of pizza, my pizza tastes better.

I'd rather eat New York pizza or good Mexican food than any fancy French cooking or nouvelle cuisine. Anytime I can't pronounce something on a menu, I don't order it. I've been to "21" in New York for lunch, but I wasn't comfortable. All the time I was sitting there, I was wishing I was over at Columbus Avenue having a pizza. Or over at Gyro III on Seventh Avenue near Madison Square Garden, having a Greek sandwich on pita bread. Or in Wolf's Deli on West Fifty-seventh Street having a corned-beef sandwich on rye with a kosher pickle.

To me, a good sandwich is a great meal. When I'm home, I like to make a tuna-fish and cheese on whole wheat bread. And for old times' sake, I'll make the only sandwich that John Robinson and I could afford when we were at the University of Oregon together: peanut butter, mayonnaise, and lettuce. It only cost fifteen cents in the cafeteria. Hey, we couldn't afford a hamburger. We couldn't even afford a bologna sandwich.

Something else I make is stew. Back in grammar school, at Our Lady of Perpetual Help in Daly City, every Tuesday the woman who cooked in the cafeteria, Mrs. Steele, made stew. Thick, brown, beef stew. The other kids hated it, but I loved it. And because I loved her stew, Mrs. Steele loved me. She always ladled out as much as I wanted, three or four helpings. You seldom see beef stew on a menu anymore. And if it's on there, it's usually too watery. It should be thick. The idea is to take all day. You can't make stew fast. I cook the onions and peppers with the meat, then I put in the potatoes and the carrots and any other vegetables that are around. I use cayenne pepper, but not tabasco. You let it simmer, you let it stew. Then you use enough flour to thicken the gravy—really thicken it.

When the stew is ready, you cut up a loaf of French bread. That's all you need for a great meal.

What I eat usually depends on where I am. If I'm on the bus, I'll throw something in the microwave or I'll ask Willie to watch for the next truckstop. If I'm in an NFL city, I've always got a favorite place. In Philadelphia I go to Pat's for cheese-steak sandwiches. Thinly sliced steak that's cooked with onions with a cheese sauce. In Chicago I go to the Billy Goat Tavern and Grill on North Michigan Avenue's lower level, down where the trucks unload. The place John Belushi and Dan Akroyd made famous on their *Saturday Night Live* skits. Near the heavy red metal door is a small sign: BUTT IN ANYTIME. Alongside the bar are small tables with red-and-white checked tablecloths. But there are no waiters or waitresses. You line up at a counter to order a burger or a sandwich off the big menu on the wall. If you ask for french fries or a Pepsi, you're in trouble.

"No fries; chips," the guy behind the counter will say, meaning a small bag of potato chips. "No Pepsi; Coke."

It's not fancy. You'll see truck drivers and warehouse workers in there at lunchtime. But you'll also see businessmen in pin-striped suits and women in silk dresses. No matter where I go in my travels, I try to find the little places, like Chili John's, in Green Bay, which once was downtown but is now out in a shopping mall. My favorite meal there is the Super Bowl, a huge order.

"The more meat we put in our chili, the more spices we put in," says Dan Hoehne, the owner. "That's how we can make it as hot as anybody wants it. And you can have it with beans or with spaghetti."

In New Orleans, the famous French Quarter restaurants are usually too crowded. I go to the Gumbo Shop for gumbo and jambalaya. When Virginia and I were in New Orleans for Super Bowl XV, which the Oakland Raiders won, she enjoyed jambalaya so much that she learned how to make it. We like it with chicken and sausage, not seafood.

Not that I *never* go to good restaurants, but there are two types that I refuse to go to: one, those that are up on the top of a tall building, like Windows on the World, perched up there in one of the World Trade Center towers; and two, those that spin around slowly while you're eating. I don't want a view or a ride. I want a good meal.

My kind of restaurant serves quantity as well as quality. I don't get to Miami often, but when I do, I try to go to Joe's Stonecrab. I'm not a big seafood eater, but I love stonecrabs with mustard sauce. In Tampa, I've had a steak at Bern's, where the wine list looks like a Bible, and I've had paella at the Café Seville, one of Pat Summerall's favorite places. In San Diego, I eat at George Pernicano's Casa di Bafi, which translates to The House of the Mustache. George has a twirled mustache long enough to rope a calf. He also has the best pork chops I've ever tasted. I never order pork chops anywhere else. I don't even like pork chops. But his pork chops are different. They're so different I've sometimes wondered if they're beef chops.

San Diego is where I learned to appreciate Mexican food. I liked it as a kid, but when I was an assistant coach at San Diego State, another coach, Sid Hall, took me to Mattia's, a great Old Town restaurant.

"Anyplace in California, it's easy to find the best Mexican restaurant," Sid told me. "Just go to the old part of town. That's where the best Mexican restaurant always is, like Mattia's. In the old part of town."

When we went on recruiting trips together to small California towns, Sid's theory never failed. No matter where we were, he always found the best Mexican restaurant. When it was time for us to eat, you could almost feel him smelling out the best Mexican restaurant in the old part of town. I use that theory now. One time I stopped in Bakersfield with some CBS guys who wanted to eat Mexican food.

"Where's the best Mexican restaurant?" one of them asked me.

"I don't know," I said, "but we'll use the Sid Hall theory."

It worked. It always does. But don't expect margaritas. If you hear somebody say, "I know a great Mexican restaurant, they have great margaritas," go somewhere else.

Unless you just want margaritas. But if you want good Mexican food, go to a restaurant where they put in the time on the food, not the margaritas. The kind of Mexican restaurant I like doesn't even have a blender for the margaritas. The salsa doesn't have to be real hot, but it has to be flavorful. And they shouldn't use hamburger in their tacos or their burritos. Tacos should be made with shredded beef, burritos with chunks of beef. Never hamburger.

Another test is when a Mexican restaurant has *menudo,* a soup made with tripe. You know how the Jewish people are with chicken soup? Jewish penicillin, they call it. No matter what's wrong with you, a Jewish mother's chicken soup will fix you up. Well, the Mexicans are like that with *menudo.* If you've got a cold or a headache, have some *menudo.*

I always like old-fashioned diners. Good food, good service. But the fast-food restaurants have all but put the diners out of business. Of all the fast-food places, my favorite is Popeye's Chicken. Not so much the chicken, but the red beans and rice. In some cities, I'll phone a good restaurant for a take-out order. Especially for barbecue in Dallas or Kansas City, where it's almost as good as in Everett & Jones in Oakland. Another good city for barbecue is Denver, but my favorite meal there is the Buffalo chicken wings that the Broncos' director of video operations, Rusty Nail, puts out for the players each Friday after practice. Rusty knows how to cook. He grew up in his mother's bakery in Winslow, Arkansas, and he once thought about going to chef's school. He uses about a hundred pounds of chicken wings, usually twenty-two to the pound, and spreads on the same hot sauce that the Anchor Bar in Buffalo uses to create their Buffalo chicken wings. Nobody's ever counted, but Rubin Carter, now the Broncos' defensive line coach after twelve seasons as their nose tackle, is considered to be their chicken-wing champ.

"Rubin usually has two or three plates," Rusty says. "That's anywhere from fifty to seventy-five wings."

I've never counted mine either, but Rusty knows I eat my share. "When I know you're coming," he once told me, "I always order an extra twenty pounds of wings." If he does, it never goes to waste. Neither does any of the celery with cheese, the pickles, or the potato salad.

"Everything just disappears," Rusty says. "Except for all the plates of bones."

But no matter what I'm eating, chicken wings or chili, I keep eating until I'm full. I don't save any room for dessert. Even as a kid, I always enjoyed the food so much that I just kept eating it until I was full. But for a snack, I've always liked ice cream. I just don't eat as much of it as I did when Ice Cream Land in Daly City put up a twenty-five–dollar prize for the person who ate the most ice cream that week.

It was easy to win the money. The contest ended every Saturday night, so I'd just wait until about an hour before closing time. Then whatever the leading amount of scoops was, I'd just sit there and eat enough to top it. Anywhere from forty to fifty scoops.

The secret was not to go for the fancy flavors. Some kids ordered chocolate with chocolate topping and whipped cream. If you were serious about winning the twenty-five dollars, like I was, it's easier to eat basic vanilla. But after a few weeks of handing me twenty-five dollars every night, the owner of Ice Cream Land made me an offer.

"I need a guy behind the counter," he said. "You get a dollar an hour and all the ice cream you can eat."

I took the job. But after a couple of weeks I realized he had conned me. I had all the ice cream I could eat, but I wasn't getting the free twenty-five dollars a week anymore.

POKER

Of all the things I do to relax, I'd rather play poker than anything else. It's not for the money. I don't want to lose any money, but I don't want anybody else's money either. It's just the winning and the losing. And most of all, it's the camaraderie. You've got talk. You've got kidding. There's nothing like having six or seven guys sitting around a table playing poker. For me, it's the game, not the gambling.

I've never been much of a gambler. When I go to Las Vegas or Atlantic City now to see a fight, I don't roll dice and I don't play blackjack, roulette, or the slot machines. But if there's a big poker game going on in the card room of the casino, I'll watch. Years ago, when Virginia and I used to drive over to Vegas in our little Volkswagen four times a year for a quick vacation, I would sit in the poker game at The Dunes all afternoon and always win around twenty or thirty dollars, enough then to pay for dinner and a show. But now I usually play poker only with some of the CBS guys, like Pat Summerall, Bob Stenner, Sandy Grossman, and Richie Zyontz, or with some of my old Pleasanton neighbors, like Carl the Cop, Floyd the Barber, and Larry Plisskin.

We don't play for much money, usually one and two dollars. I don't think anybody ever wins or loses much. I just enjoy the camaraderie of being with guys I like, and I enjoy the game itself. I like the quickness of it, deciding whether to play a card or not play a card.

When we were first married, Virginia was teaching English at Santa Maria High School and I was teaching Phys. Ed. and coaching football at Hancock Junior College, so our trips to Vegas had to coincide with the school vacations. We went when school got out in June, and again in August just before school resumed. We also went during our Christmas and Easter vacations. As soon as we checked in at The Dunes, Virginia would go sit by the swimming pool and I'd go sit in a poker game. Five-card stud.

I never made a big killing at The Dunes, maybe thirty-five dollars on my best day, but I can't remember ever losing any money. And that's not bragging. That's patience.

In all those poker games I learned that if you were patient, you could always win. Maybe not much, but in Vegas I wasn't trying to win much. In those years, Vegas was really inexpensive. Our room at The Dunes, as I remember, was something like twelve bucks a night. Dinner and a show weren't much more than that. One of the first times Virginia and I went to Vegas, we were standing at the end of a long line waiting to see Don Rickles, when I noticed a hotel usher at a side door.

"Can we slip through that door?" I asked.

"That depends," he said with a big wink.

I slipped him ten dollars and he motioned us through the side door. "You want to sit up front?" he said.

"Yeah, sure," I said. "Great."

"You got a lot of guts," he snapped.

I thought the usher was getting on me for sneaking in the side door, but almost as soon as Rickles got on stage he picked me out to be the "fat queer" for that show. Hey, he was funny. I laughed like hell at him, and at myself. But whenever Virginia and I went to see him after that, we sat in the back where he couldn't spot me.

Vegas is different now. In the glitzy casino-hotels, room prices are high. Dinners and shows are expensive. But in those years when Vegas was trying to establish itself, the casino-hotels attracted you with those low prices. They almost gave away the room, the food, and the shows, in return for you just being there. They figured that enough people would lose enough money gambling for the casinos to come out ahead.

With most people, that's how it usually worked. They'd lose a few bucks. Sometimes big bucks. Most people try to force a winning hand, but that's the worst mistake you can make. Instead, play your cards compared to the other cards. If something's not there, don't try to manufacture it. Let somebody else win that hand, then you try to win the next hand. You hear people say, "I'm hot" or "I'm getting good cards." Or you hear them moan, "I'm getting bad cards." But if you play long enough, you're going to get some good cards *and* bad cards.

With me, basically, it's play the hell out of the good cards, and don't try to play the bad cards. It's like Kenny Rogers sings, "You gotta know when to hold 'em and know when to fold 'em." Do that and you'll usually win.

In those poker games at The Dunes, I had the advantage of knowing I had all afternoon to wait for good cards. Sooner or later, those good cards appeared. If you're patient, they always do. In those games, the table had seven seats, but you only needed five guys to get the game going. The house provided the dealer, but he didn't play, he just dealt. To get the game started, the house also provided enough house men to sit in as players, but as soon as a live customer wanted to sit in, a house man got up. I played there often enough in those years that I got to know the dealers. The owner of The Dunes, Sid Wyman, even got to know me.

"Hey, big guy," he said to me once, "if you're interested, we got bigger games than this."

I wasn't interested. I was just there to make enough money for dinner and a show that night and, if I got a little lucky, to pay our room bill. But late in the afternoon, after I'd made my stake for the day, I'd wander over to where the bigger games were. On the table were a pile of those black hundred-dollar chips, or sometimes a pile of hundred-dollar bills. Just seeing all that money made my hands sweat. Those guys would be playing for ten thousand a card, and they'd call.

No matter how much money I had, I remember thinking then, *I could never do that.*

I still couldn't play poker in those big games. And when I go to a big fight now, in Vegas or Atlantic City, I don't play poker at all. In Vegas, I prefer to sit in the Caesars Palace Sports Book, watching the different ballgames on all the television screens. That's a great place to hang out. One time a guy from Iowa told me he was spending his two-week vacation betting games in the Sports Book there.

"Don't you go to a show?" I asked.

"Nope," he said, "I just sit here and bet the races, the baseball games, whatever they got."

"Don't you go out to the pool?"

"Nope, I just sit here and bet the races and the ballgames for two weeks."

"That's your vacation?"

"Yep," he said. "That's my two-week vacation."

"What'd you do on your vacation last year?"

"Same thing I'm doing now."

"What're you gonna do on your vacation next year?"

"Same thing I'm doing now."

That's his thing, I guess. Just like poker is my thing.

NEW YORK, NEW YORK

henever I spend some time in New York between NFL games, I stay in an apartment on the West Side, which isn't that different from Daly City, where I grew up. On the West Side the fruit stands, the little storefronts and the restaurants create the same feeling I always had in Daly City of living in a neighborhood.

When I walk around the West Side, it's almost like I've been there before. I buy the papers at the corner newsstand. I buy apples and peaches. I buy a glass of freshly squeezed orange juice. I'm just glad I'm not a little kid growing up there, because the difference between the West Side and almost any other neighborhood in America is that there are hardly any little kids. You see a few, but not many. All the New York people with little kids must live in the suburbs or the other boroughs. What you do see on the West Side is a lot of old people, mostly old ladies. When I first stayed there, I saw old ladies in cloth coats in a Greek coffee shop every morning, just sipping their coffee and picking on a piece of toast. They'd be there for hours. Maybe that's why that coffee shop went out of business. There's a pizza place there now; I don't see those old ladies anymore. They probably found another coffee shop.

When the weather is nice, I like to walk around the neighborhood. Over to Broadway, up and down Columbus Avenue. Anywhere I go I usually walk. I seldom take a taxi. I've never been in the subway.

I've never even driven a car in New York, but that's not a boast. To me, New York has the best drivers anywhere. For all that traffic, I've never seen an accident. Not even a fender-bender. Hey, accidents happen in New York, just like anywhere else, but personally I've never seen one. You see people hurrying across streets and you see cars and taxis zooming along, but I've never seen 'em collide. I've heard brakes screech, but no crashes. I've seen tow trucks pulling a car out of a "no parking" zone, but I've never seen a tow truck for an accident. When I'm traveling in my bus out in the middle of nowhere, I'll sometimes see a tow truck at an accident, but not in New York.

"Why is that?" I asked one of our Greyhound drivers. "All this space out here on an interstate, and there's an accident. All that traffic in New York, and I never see an accident."

"Concentration," he said. "In that New York traffic, people concentrate more. Out on an empty Interstate, people daydream, especially in the daytime. At night, people concentrate better."

There's another thing about New York traffic: almost every driver is a professional—a taxi driver, a bus driver. Even the commuter driver is virtually a professional. I know people who refuse to drive in New York, but that's good. If those people are that concerned about surviving in New York traffic, chances are they'd be so nervous, they'd be in an accident. All those professional drivers are another reason New York works.

Think about it. If you put all those people in all those buildings in Manhattan, then tried to get on and off Manhattan island every day, feeding them at lunchtime, if you had to start from scratch to do this, it would never come out right. But somehow, New York works. Every time I walk around the West Side, it never ceases to amaze me.

I usually can't watch other people because it ends up with them watching me. Sometimes that happens on the West Side too. One night outside my apartment, a guy in a baseball cap came by. He was wearing a windbreaker, jeans, and tennis shoes, just like dozens of other people out on the street. He glanced over at me and did a double-take. That's the problem with my size. You can't blend into the background. When you're my size, you are the foreground. Anyway, this guy in the baseball cap walked over and we talked for maybe an hour. Nice guy, interesting guy. We talked about the Giants and the Jets, we talked about baseball, then he asked me if I had seen the television spot that John Candy, the comedian, had done in an art gallery with a chalkboard.

"I heard about it," I said, "but I missed it."

"The producer is a friend of mine," he said. "I'll have him send you a copy."

"Hey, that's nice of you to do that," I said.

"By the way," he said, "my name's Paul Simon."

Another time I was walking down Columbus Avenue when I recognized a little guy in a raincoat walking the other way. I guess he recognized me, too. He looked at me and held up his right thumb, so I held up my right thumb. But he just kept on walking. Dustin Hoffman.

After he walked by, I turned to see if anybody else recognized him. But nobody did. That's an advantage little guys have.

Some days I go over into Central Park and sit on a bench. Usually nobody notices me there, but one day an ambulance stopped and two guys got out and walked over to me. Football fans, it turned out. Giants fans.

"How come," one guy asked me, "you're so nice to Phil Simms?"

There I was, minding my own business, just sitting on a bench in Central Park, midway through the 1986 season, and two guys hop out of an ambulance to ask me why I'm "so nice" to Phil Simms.

"Nice?" I said.

"Yeah," the other guy said. "You're always saying that he's one of the best quarterbacks in the NFL."

"He is," I said. "He is one of the best."

"Ahhh," one said, "he ain't that good."

"Hey, I'm not being nice to him," I said. "That's just what I think of him and of what he's doing."

"Ahhh," the other said.

I couldn't convince them. But in Super Bowl XXI maybe Phil Simms convinced them. It's strange how fans will like some players immediately, and dislike others immediately. The day the Giants chose Phil Simms in the first round, in 1979, the fans who always attend the NFL draft in New York booed him. Some fans still boo him.

Don't ask me to explain why. Maybe it's because he has blond hair. Or because he came out of Morehead State in Kentucky, a college hardly anybody has heard of. Or because he happened to be the quarterback on several bad Giants teams, when he wasn't hurt.

That's typical of many New York fans. Whatever the sport, a player is either a hero or a bum, depending on his last game. That's true in most cities, but even more so in New York.

Most days in Central Park, I just watch the people pass by. Try to figure out where they're from, where they're going, what they're doing. And then there are the homeless people. You see these people, most of them old, with all their belongings in a shopping bag, sometimes a shopping cart. That's it. That's all they own. They sleep curled up on the hard wooden benches or in the bushes. And every morning the cops come by to check on them.

"Are you OK?" I've heard cops ask.

"I'm OK," that person would mumble.

If the person looked and sounded OK, the cop would go on to the next person. But if anybody didn't look right, or was hungry or needed clothes, the cop would take them to a city shelter. In the winter months, as soon as the temperature drops below freezing, cops are under orders to take the homeless to a shelter. But if they're healthy, most homeless people don't want to go to a shelter. To them, that park bench or those bushes are their home. In that respect, they're just like you and me. Nobody wants to be taken out of their home.

"No, no," I've heard some of those people yell at a cop, "don't you touch me."

I'm not in New York that much, but I think I see more of it than most New Yorkers do. Between bus trips, I just hang out. That lets me watch the people in New York without my really being a part of New York itself. I'm like a fly on a wall there, on a West Side wall. I seldom go to other parts of the city. Once in a while Virginia and I will go to dinner over on the East Side, or down in Greenwich Village, and I've gone to Brooklyn for a steak at Peter Luger's restaurant. But if I go out for dinner in those places, I've got to dress up. On the West Side I can go anywhere in a sweat suit and sneakers.

I don't go to the museums or the ballet. I don't go to the theater. I not only don't go to the theater, I don't even pronounce it correctly. I call it thee-ay-ter, which always annoys Virginia, but she knows better than to ask me to go with her to the thee-ay-ter. The only time I ever went was in 1959, when I was a rookie with the Philadelphia Eagles. My roommate was Darrel Aschbacher, a guard from the University of Oregon. He decided we needed a little New York culture.

"On our day off," he said, "let's go up to New York on the train and see *Fiddler on the Roof.*"

As soon as we got off the train in Penn Station, I knew I had made a mistake. Here we were, me from California and Darrel from Oregon, two hicks in the big city. When we got inside the theater, I knew I had made another mistake. The seat was too small for me. Much too small. Even the theater itself was small. Claustrophobia was closing in on me. Almost as soon as the curtain went up on *Fiddler on the Roof,* I started glancing at my watch to see if it was almost over. I'm the same way about movies, not just in New York, but anywhere. There's something about that commitment to two hours that I don't want to make, especially in little dark theaters. One night I was having dinner with Dick Stockton, the CBS announcer, and his wife, Lesley Visser, who's a *Boston Globe* sportswriter. Lesley started asking me what I do in New York.

"I just hang out," I said.

"Haven't you been to the theater?" she asked.

"Once, in 1959."

"Don't you ever go to the opera, or the ballet at Lincoln Center? You can walk there."

"No."

"How about a museum?" she said. "The Museum of Natural History is just up the street from where you live. And the Metropolitan Museum of Art is just across Central Park. Haven't you been to those museums?"

"No."

When people ask me about it, I'm not going to con them. I've never been to those places, and I don't particularly want to go. I was thinking about taking the *QE 2* to Europe a couple of summers ago, but then I happened to mention it to some of my friends.

"What," one of them asked, "are you going to do when you get over there?"

"I haven't really thought about that yet," I said. "What do you do when you go to Europe?"

"You visit museums?"

"I don't go to museums. I've got two great museums in New York that I can walk to, and I don't go. What else can you do?"

"You sightsee?"

"I don't even do that here," I said. "I've been in Washington dozens of times, but I've never gone to the Smithsonian or the White House or the Capitol building. And all the time I've spent in New York, I've never been to the Statue of Liberty or the United Nations, or to the top of the Empire State Building or the World Trade Center."

The more I thought about it, the more I realized it didn't make much sense for me to go all the way to Europe on the *QE 2* to visit museums that I didn't want to visit.

Hey, it's not just museums with old paintings and old dinosaurs. It can be a museum with old football players. I went to George Blanda's induction into the Pro Football Hall of Fame in Canton, Ohio, in 1981, but after walking through one wing of the Hall of Fame, with all those bronze busts, that was enough for me.

I just prefer live people and live things. Maybe that's why I'm so comfortable in New York.

BOSS

ver since Virginia and I got married, we've almost always had English bulldogs around the house. Sometimes we've had two or three at a time, like we do now with Tug, Moose, and Missy. Overall we've had seven, plus a few litters. Our first bulldog was a puppy who was asleep in a pet store in 1960. Virginia heard him snoring.

"I had to buy him," Virginia told me. "He sounded just like you do when you snore. Very soothing."

Most people don't like the sound of snoring, but Virginia really does find it soothing, at least mine she does. We named the puppy Pug, and when we wanted to breed her two years later, we got Peter. After they had a litter, we kept Dapper Dan, a female who was so ugly we called her by a male name so she wouldn't feel bad.

"Dapper Dan died in 1976," Virginia always recalls, "the day we beat New England in the playoffs."

That's the way the wife of a Raider coach remembers dates—in relation to football games. And after Dapper Dan died, we didn't have a bulldog for about a year. We tried a couple of "cockapoos," a cross between a cocker spaniel and a poodle, but they weren't the same.

"I wish we had a bulldog," I kept saying.

Around that time, Virginia thought I was treating our son Joe too much like a baby. Joe was twelve then, and Virginia decided that if we had another bulldog, I'd stop treating Joe like a baby and treat the dog like a baby. That's when Virginia and Joe picked out Boss, the bulldog who will always be special to me.

Boss was big for a bulldog, about sixty pounds. His ancestors were bred to bait bulls, and Boss didn't get short-changed on genes. He had that classic bulldog face, with the protruding lower lip. Ugly but handsome.

Some people always joked that Boss looked like Winston Churchill, but then everybody thinks every English bulldog looks like Winston Churchill. Hey, if Boss had been human, he'd have been Lawrence Taylor, the Giants' linebacker. Boss was a good dog, but sometimes he was a little left of the rail. No matter how good he was most of the time, you never knew when he was going to erupt. Every so often he chewed up whatever was in the backyard—hoses, a chunk of the diving board, a slab of fence. One time, after he chewed through our fence, he went into our neighbor's backyard and chewed up some things. They had Boss thrown in the dog pound. The next thing we knew, we got a police citation.

"Boss Madden," it read. "At large."

That wasn't his only citation. Some people put pictures of their kids on the refrigerator. We put Boss's citations up there. Another time Boss took on a gardener's power edger, the tool that clips the edge of the grass next to the sidewalk and the driveway. Not a hand-tool, a power tool. The edger was buzzing when Boss attacked it with his mouth; attacked it and stopped it. He chewed the edger to a stop. His mouth was all blood, but he didn't care. He had stopped that edger.

Another time, when we were in our New York apartment, Virginia took Boss over to Central Park for a walk. Boss noticed a street person on one of the benches and pulled Virginia that way. Virginia thought Boss was hoping to be petted, but when Boss got to the street person, he lifted his leg.

Mike and Joe would play rough with Boss, but when Boss's growl got deeper, they knew it was time to back off. Everybody who was around Boss knew enough to be careful. Even me, even Virginia, even the boys. Boss had that linebacker look about him. Once when I took him for a walk, I heard a woman calling to me from a taxi cab.

"You're not going to get your big ass mugged, are you?" she yelled.

Sue Simmons, the anchorwoman who had interviewed me on the *Live at Five* show on Channel 4 in New York, had spotted Boss, who would deter any sensible mugger. Strangers were usually wary of Boss—so much so that whenever strangers were around the house, I made sure Boss wasn't. One day in 1985 a photographer stopped by our house in Pleasanton to take some pictures of me in the backyard for a Drexel Burnham ad.

"Let me put Boss in his pen," I said.

"No, I like him," the photographer said.

"You sure?" I asked.

"I like him," he said.

They got along. When the photographer was through shooting me, he took some pictures of Boss with me.

"I'll send you the pictures," he said.

Instead of mailing them to me directly, he mailed them to Jean Sage, an agent at IMG, who had arranged the photo session. As soon as Jean saw the photos, she phoned me.

"Have you ever thought," she asked, "about using Boss in television commercials?"

Jean had it all figured out how Boss would be perfect for a dog-food commercial. And whatever money Boss made, I was going to put in a bank account under the name of Boss Madden, and use it to pay for all the hoses, fences, diving boards, and whatever else he destroyed. By then Boss and Tug (a female we got in 1980 when Tug McGraw was a World Series hero for the Philadelphia Phillies) had produced a litter that included Moose and Missy. Several days after Jean talked about a TV commercial for Boss, she phoned.

"I've got the commercial," she said.

"You won't believe this, but Boss died yesterday," I said. "The vet told us he had some form of cancer in his intestines. He was so tough, we never suspected anything until we found him."

I've never thought of using any of our other English bulldogs in a commercial. There was only one like Boss.

"THIS IS RONALD REAGAN"

I see Jack Kemp every so often at a football game or a football dinner, but when we talk it's always about when we were in the American Football League together. Or it's about his son Jeff, who's been a quarterback with several NFL teams. But we never talk politics. Jack Kemp wants to be president of the United States someday, and for his sake I hope he's elected. But long before he was a Congressman from the Buffalo area, he was the Bills' quarterback. And a good one. But now *he's* a politician, and *I'm* anything but.

The only thing I know about politics is that I don't know enough about it to talk about it intelligently.

I've always thought that just because somebody is a good athlete or a good coach or a good anything else, that doesn't make him an expert on politics. He's entitled to his opinion on a candidate or an issue, but he shouldn't go around spouting his opinion, because it's probably not an educated opinion. When you talk publicly about something as important as national or state—or even local—politics, you have a responsibility to know what you're talking about. I've never thought that just because I coached the Oakland Raiders or do NFL games for CBS I have a right to talk politics. (My only theory on politics is that whenever somebody runs for president, they should take a trip across the country on the ground, not fly from airport to airport.)

If you try to be an expert on a subject in which you have no expertise, it's a mistake. You're better off keeping your mouth shut. Otherwise, everybody is going to discover how much you *don't* know.

As you can see, I don't exactly consider myself an adviser to the president, which is why the experience I had on March 5, 1987, was somewhat shocking. It was the day after President Reagan had talked to the nation on television about the Iran–contra controversy. I had driven to the Pleasanton Hilton for lunch with Steve Gilmour and Dennis Garrison, who own the hotel. I had just ordered a Thai chicken salad when the hostess came over.

"Mr. Madden," she said, "please call Larry Plisskin at your office."

I looked around for a phone. "I'll get one," Steve said, "and we'll plug it in here." I knew something was up. Larry Plisskin is a real-estate broker who works out of my office, but he had never phoned me at lunch before. No matter how important something was, Larry knew it could wait until I got back to the office. But obviously this couldn't wait. After Steve got the phone plugged in and I called Larry, I knew why.

"The White House is trying to get you," Larry said. "Chuck Bennett has the details."

The White House? What does the White House want with me? I phoned Chuck Bennett, a vice president in the International Management Group office in New York.

"The president wants to talk to you," Chuck said. "Give me the phone number where you are."

I gave Chuck the number, then I looked over at Steve and Dennis, who didn't know what to think.

"Can you make sure the phones work around here?" I said. "The President is going to call me."

Steve grabbed the phone, gave the hotel operator our extension, and had her ring us back. Then we sat there staring at the phone. When our food came, we started eating. But nobody was saying anything. We kept staring at the phone, waiting for it to ring. Finally, it did. "It's for you, John," Dennis said, handing me the phone. "It's the White House."

"Hello," I said. "Hello?"

"This is White House operator 2 for John Madden," a woman's voice said. "Is this John Madden?"

"This is he," I said.

Another woman's voice came on the phone. "President Reagan is calling for John Madden. Is this John Madden?"

"Yes."

"Are you ready to talk to the president?"

"Yes."

I really wasn't ready. I mean, how do you get ready to talk to the president? Talking to the operators, I had been sitting down, but now I decided to stand up. But even standing up, I wasn't ready. I'd never met President Reagan, never talked to him. Never met or talked to any president. When the Raiders won Super Bowl XI, the president was Gerald Ford, who didn't phone the winning coach. I'd finally won the Super Bowl, but I had a president who didn't phone.

"Hello, John," I heard now, "this is Ronald Reagan."

The night before, after the president's televised speech about the Iran–contra situation, the newswoman kept calling him "Mr. Reagan," which came as a surprise to me. I always thought he should be called "President Reagan" or "Mr. President." So now, when I heard his voice, my first thought was, *I don't know what to call him!* I had thought one of his aides would come on the phone before he did. When he said, "Hello, John, this is Ronald Reagan," I didn't want to call him anything that might be wrong, so I just blurted out:

"Hi, how ya doin'?"

He didn't seem to mind. He told me about a Hollywood friend of his, a motion-picture producer who was going to produce some public-service television spots for the Space Program, using two very different guys.

"Kareem Abdul-Jabbar with Willie Shoemaker," the president explained. "They won't see eye to eye."

I didn't know enough to laugh. At least not until a few seconds later, when I probably sounded stupid. But by then he was telling me about the spot that *I* was supposed to do.

"Chuck Yeager will be with you," he said. "Fly and no fly. How does that sound to you?"

"That sounds great," I said, still not calling him anything that might be wrong. "I'll be glad to do it."

"Thank you, John," he said. "They'll be in touch with you."

"Thank you," I said. "That spot sounds like a lot of fun."

We talked some more, but when I thought about it later, I wondered why one of the president's aides didn't call me about that TV spot. The president had just given that speech to the nation the night before about the Iran–contra thing, and all I could picture was a line on his schedule for today.

"Call John Madden," it said.

I didn't know how to address the president, but at least I didn't say something I shouldn't have. I mumbled my way through a similar experience one morning in late December 1985, just after I had bought the New York morning papers at the newsstand on the corner of West Seventy-second Street and Columbus Avenue, down the block from my apartment. I was crossing Seventy-second Street when I heard a man's voice.

"Mr. Madden," I heard, "Mr. Madden."

I turned and saw the driver of a big black sedan, a Cadillac or a Lincoln as I remember. He beckoned me toward the car.

"President Nixon," he said, "would like to say hello."

I looked over at the car. Richard Nixon was the only other person in it, and he was sitting on the passenger's side of the front seat. That impressed me. I always assumed that an ex-president would be in the back seat if he had a driver. But this ex-president was up there in the front seat, just like anybody else.

"That was quite a game yesterday," he said.

The day before, the Giants had knocked the 49ers out of the NFC playoffs, 17–3, at Giants Stadium. Now the Giants had to go to Chicago to play the Bears.

"I'm a Giant fan," he said, "but I don't think they can beat the Bears."

"I don't think so, either," I told him. "I think the Bears will win the Super Bowl."

"I'm afraid you're right," he said.

I knew he was a football fan. When he was president, he followed the Redskins closely. When the Dolphins were going to play the Cowboys in Super Bowl VI, he phoned Don Shula to suggest a "down and in" pass from Bob Griese to Paul Warfield. The play didn't work and the Dolphins lost, 24–3, but at least the Dolphins had the president rooting for them.

"He told me he was a Redskin fan," Shula said at the time. "But he liked the Dolphins because he was a part-time resident of Miami."

The day of our conversation, Richard Nixon was a full-time resident of northern New Jersey, which I assume is why he had become attached to the Giants. But he knew his football. He had already figured out why the Bears would be too good for the Giants.

"I'd like to see the Giants win," he said, "but the Bears' defense will handle the Giants' offense."

That's exactly what happened, 21–0. He had called it. And for about fifteen minutes that day, he talked football like a man who knew what he was talking about.

"I enjoyed this, John," he finally said, "but I've got to go."

And that's the extent of my life in politics—except for the time when I checked into the Four Seasons hotel in Washington, late on the Friday night before the Redskins played the 49ers for the 1983 NFC championship. As I signed the register, the room clerk handed me one of those pink telephone-message slips.

"Please call Ethel Kennedy," it read. "You don't have to comb your hair."

During the Redskins' 51–7 rout of the Rams the week before, Dick Vermeil was about to go on camera with Brent Musberger at halftime, when I noticed Dick combing his hair. I turned to Pat Summerall.

"I've never carried a comb in my life," I said. "I only comb my hair once a day. In the morning. That's all."

So when I saw this telephone message from Ethel Kennedy with the note about combing my hair I assumed it was a phoney. It sounded like something Bob Stenner would pull. But on the message it also said that operator 5 took it. I figured I better check with operator 5, so I got the switchboard and asked operator 5 about this message from Ethel Kennedy.

"Did some guy call?" I asked.

"No, that was Mrs. Kennedy," the operator said.

"How do you know?"

"I know her voice."

Uh-oh, now I've got to return the call. It was too late to call that night, but the next morning I dialed the number on the message slip. Ethel Kennedy answered the phone.

"John," she said, "we're having a party tonight and we'd like you to come. And you don't have to comb your hair."

I thanked her, but I begged off. I told her I had to work but my real reason was I didn't have the proper clothes with me. When you see me doing a game in the CBS booth, I'm wearing a blue blazer over a tie and shirt, but you don't see my old khaki pants and sneakers. From the waist down, I just wear whatever happens to be around. Even if I didn't have to comb my hair for Ethel Kennedy's party, I wasn't about to show up in sneakers.

WHY I CHEW
CIGARS

I buy cigars by the box. Good cigars. Because a cheap cigar falls apart. But I don't smoke those good cigars. I just chew 'em. I don't smoke at all. Not anymore.

As a kid, I never smoked. Not in high school, not in college. But when I was in a Philadelphia hospital after my knee operation in 1959, I started smoking cigarettes. I was a rookie guard with the Eagles that year. In a training camp scrimmage, I was blocking on a running play when the tackler drove the ball carrier across the back of my left knee. Torn ligaments. Out for the season. Out for my career. In the hospital, I asked for a pack of cigarettes to ease the pain, to ease the tension. After that, I just kept smoking. When I started coaching at Allan Hancock Junior College in Santa Maria, California, and later at San Diego State, I smoked even more. By the time I was the Raiders' coach, I was up to a pack a day. If I had a long day, maybe two packs.

On game days, I even smoked on the Raiders sideline. When the television cameras zoomed in on me, sometimes I was grabbing a quick puff.

The more the cameras picked me up, the more letters I got, mostly from kids and parents. "You shouldn't smoke, it's bad for your lungs," the kids wrote. "You shouldn't smoke," the parents wrote, "you're setting a bad example." At first, I thought they were just cranky people. But the more letters I got, the more I realized they were right and I was wrong. I stopped smoking on the sideline, and I started to cut down. I went to those *light* cigarettes, lighter and lighter, but I didn't stop. Then one night in 1983, I was sitting with Virginia in Bob's Big Boy restaurant near our Pleasanton home. I was about to light a cigarette when I heard two older guys talking near the cash register.

"I've got to quit smoking," I heard one say. "The doctor tells me it's going to kill me."

"You're lucky it hasn't killed you by now," the other guy said. "How many heart attacks have you had?"

"Two, and two open-heart operations. The doctor's right. Smoking is going to kill me."

Instead of lighting my cigarette, I crushed it into the ashtray. I thought, *I don't need this anymore,* but I didn't say anything to Virginia, who still smoked then. I didn't want to say anything to anybody just yet, because if I announced that I had quit smoking and then lit one up ten minutes later, everybody would laugh at me. But when Virginia tossed me a cigarette the next morning in the kitchen, I tossed it back.

"I don't smoke anymore," I said.

"When did you stop?" she said.

"Last night," I said. "I heard a guy talking about all his heart operations and heart attacks."

"What guy?"

"I don't know who he was. I just know that I don't want to go through what he's been through."

"Can you make it stick?"

"I'll make it stick."

Two years later Virginia stopped. But as soon as I crushed that cigarette into the ashtray in Bob's Big Boy that night, I didn't want another cigarette. When I woke up the next morning, I didn't want one. But when the phone rang later that day, I realized I was looking for a cigarette. I had developed a habit of picking up the phone, grabbing a cigarette, and smoking while I talked on the phone. I knew I had to find a way to cope with that urge when the phone rang. That's when I went to chewing a cigar. Not smoking it. Just chewing it.

OUR TWO SONS

There's no trick to raising kids. It's strictly work. Day-to-day work. With our two sons growing up when I was the Raiders' coach, Virginia did most of the work. She did it well. Mike is a 1987 Harvard graduate with a major in English who's working for the International Management Group now as an account executive. Joe will be graduating from Brown in 1989 with a major in Organizational Behavioral Management. And they're both good kids.

As their father, I like to think I had a little input in raising them. I've always believed in doing two things with kids. One is getting them to enjoy what they're doing now; the other is encouraging them, but not rushing them.

It's never easy for kids to enjoy what they're doing. From the time children are born until they graduate from college, adults are always rushing them into the future. When is the baby going to walk? When is the baby going to talk? When is the baby going to recite ABC's? As soon as the child starts grammar school, adults start asking, "Where are you going to high school?" When a teenager is in high school, they ask, "Where are you going to college?" When a college kid starts freshman year, they ask, "What are you majoring in?" And finally, they ask, "What are you going to do when you graduate?"

By that time, some kids have been so busy worrying about where they're going that they never had time to enjoy where they've been.

When our boys were small, I told them to enjoy grammar school. As they got older, I told them to enjoy high school and to enjoy college. Hey, they knew that didn't mean I wanted them to enjoy school by goofing off. The best way to enjoy school is by getting good marks. That way, your parents and your teachers aren't nagging you to get good marks. I know. I didn't work hard in school until I was going for my master's degree in Education. When I talked to our boys about their schoolwork, Virginia reminded me that *I* had not been a serious student.

"You expect them to work hard in school," she'd say, "but you didn't work hard until you went to graduate school."

True enough, but I didn't want my boys to make the same mistake I had. I was lucky. In college I didn't bother to study because I thought I'd play football forever. But then, as a rookie with the Eagles in their 1959 training camp, I had needed knee surgery. I wasn't just through for the season. I was through, period. As unlucky as that might sound now, it was the best break I've ever had. I went back to Cal Poly, got my master's, got a coaching job at Allan Hancock Junior College, moved on to San Diego State as an assistant coach, was hired by the Raiders in 1967 as a linebacker coach, was named head coach in 1969, won Super Bowl XI, won 103 games in ten seasons, decided to stop coaching, and here I am. I couldn't assume that either of my boys would be that lucky. That's why I was after them to get good marks. But, unlike some fathers, I never pushed them into sports.

If your kids don't like baseball, don't push them to play. If you do, they'll resist, because they'll think it's *your* idea. But if your kids *do* like to play baseball, encourage them. If you do, they'll respond, because they'll think it's *their* idea.

Our boys played soccer for a while, but they didn't really enjoy it, so they stopped. Mike played Little League baseball, Joe didn't play it for long. He preferred the shot put. They both played football. I've never asked them, but growing up around the Raiders as they did, they probably thought they *had* to play football. Still, they enjoyed playing football right through college. Mike was a wide receiver, Joe an offensive tackle. If they hadn't enjoyed it, I doubt if they would have continued to play it.

They grew up in a football environment, but I've found that fathers who were good athletes or good coaches don't usually push their kids into sports. Athletically, those fathers have done it. They've blocked or tackled in the NFL or in college. They've thrown or swung at a big-league fastball. They've made or blocked a jump shot in the NBA or college. Or they've coached at that level. As a result, those fathers don't need to live their life through their kids. A father who was a frustrated athlete is more likely to push his kids, hoping they will accomplish what he never did.

When our boys were small, I never even took them out into the backyard to show them football fundamentals. Maybe it's just as well.

One day, when they were older and I had stopped coaching, they had a big swinging bag in the backyard that they used as a blocking dummy. I decided to show Joe how to hit that bag and drive with his legs. But when I hit it, somehow my right hand flew up and I whacked myself in the lip. Blood all over. Some coach.

I also had a problem going to their games to see them play, especially Little League baseball games.

I wanted to see how they were doing, be a parent like the other parents. But as the Raiders' coach, I didn't want to become the event myself. Anytime I went, people would come up to take my picture and talk about football, and that wasn't fair to my boys. This was *their* game, not my game. After a while, I parked up the right-field foul line and watched the game from inside the car. Football games were tougher. You had to get out of the car to watch a football game. But when the boys were in high school, my friend Carl Marsh was an assistant coach who took the game films from the little wooden press box. He let me sit in there.

Watching my kids play, I hardly said a word. I didn't even yell at the umpires or the officials. One reason was that I didn't want to let people know I was there. But the main reason was that I didn't want to act like some of the other parents. It's one thing to yell *for* your kid's team, but it's another to yell *at* your kid. At that age, your kids have enough pressure on them, especially with their parents watching. They don't need the added pressure of hearing their parents yelling at them. Most of those parents would be better off letting their kids enjoy something outside of sports—playing the piano, collecting stamps. Anything the *kid* wants to do.

It's the same with schoolwork. If you don't enjoy French, take another language. If you don't enjoy chemistry, take physics. I'm not talking about a subject like math. Hey, you've got to know math, whether you enjoy it or not. You've got to know grammar and literature and history, whether you enjoy them or not. But with an elective subject, take what you enjoy. You'll get better marks.

Another of my theories about raising kids is, don't let them go to work until they have to go to work. My father taught me that. "You'll be working the rest of your life after you get out of school," he once told me. "Enjoy yourself until you have to go to work." That fits in with how kids should enjoy what they're doing now, instead of worrying about where they're going to high school or college, or what they're going to be. There's a time to worry about that, but until that time comes, enjoy what you're doing *now.* I think our boys enjoyed what they were doing while they were growing up, although one time, their mother got on Mike about his room.

"You don't work," Virginia said. "The least you can do is keep your room clean."

"I work," Mike said quietly. "I work at being a good kid. That's a tough job."

Mike was right, and Virginia knew it. Back when Virginia and I were kids, it was easier to be a kid. In those years, a bad kid was somebody who smoked a cigarette or drank a beer. These days, kids are confronted with some hard temptations, especially street drugs that are not only addictive but capable of killing them.

I'm not trying to canonize our boys, or Virginia and myself. The boys had their moments, and so did we. But being around the Raiders was a subject other kids didn't take in school.

From the time Mike and Joe were little boys, they were privileged. Not financially—I wasn't making much money. But they were privileged in being allowed to grow up around an NFL team. As soon as they were old enough, I took them to the Raiders training camp with me every year. They didn't come to work as ball boys, but just to hang out, to enjoy the experience.

"Any favorite players?" I asked them that first year.

"Any who talk to us are our favorites," Mike said.

Even after I stopped coaching, they continued to go to the Raiders training camp for a couple of weeks every year. As an offensive lineman, Joe has had tips from Art Shell, once an All-Pro offensive tackle and now the Raiders' offensive line coach.

"Art has really helped me with my pass-blocking," Joe told me.

Back when Dave Casper was the Raiders' tight end, the boys couldn't wait to see what he might do next. "Casper," Joe told me, "is a guy who always seems to be enjoying himself." Which is exactly what I wanted our boys to do. Maybe not quite so much as Dave Casper sometimes enjoyed himself, but he had the right idea. Even when the boys were little, I drove them to practice every Saturday before a home game. When the team was in a meeting, Mike and Joe were out on the Coliseum field, playing football with the kids of the players and the other coaches. When the Raiders practiced, all the kids watched. When the players went back to the locker room to shower and dress, the kids would play again. I'd drive them home, then drive up Saturday night to be with my team at the airport Hilton, where the players were always lodged the night before a home game. Sunday morning our neighbor, Art Williams, would usually drive the boys up to the game. Afterward, they would meet me at the team party at the Hilton. At an early age they learned the importance of competition. Once, Mike was sitting on a chartered bus next to Henry Lawrence, a Pro Bowl offensive tackle.

"Whenever you do something, Mike, you got to win," Henry said. "I don't care if you and another kid are standing there seeing how far you can pee—*you* got to pee farther than the other guy."

Another time, Mike was standing with my old boss Al Davis, on the sideline at training camp. In the weeks before the Raiders won Super Bowl XVIII, Al summed up his philosophy on life with, "Just win, baby." But he had impressed that philosophy on Mike long before that.

"You know, Michael," he said that day at training camp, "all there is in life is winning. All you have to do is win. Well, yeah, I suppose there are other things in life, but who cares?"

Mike and Joe cared. Among their other things in life was choosing a good college. By then Mike was at Choate, a Connecticut prep school, and he was thinking about going to an Ivy League college. On a visit to the Raiders training camp, I mentioned that to Bob Chandler, a wide receiver who had gone to Southern Cal.

"I wish I had gone to an Ivy League college," Chandler said. "That way I would've gotten a better education, still played football, and had time to absorb more of the college experience. Football at Southern Cal was almost a full-time job."

I was glad to hear that. Mike wasn't going to college to

prepare himself for the NFL, he was going to college for an education. And when I told Mike what Bob Chandler had said, it helped convince him to choose Harvard, where he could play football, but where football wouldn't intrude on his education and his college experience. The first time we visited Mike at Harvard, all the students were walking around like they had an Excedrin headache. Very competitive. Go, go, go. But when Mike got along well in that atmosphere, it influenced Joe to choose Brown, another Ivy League college. Brown doesn't seem to be quite as competitive as Harvard, so it fit Joe better. Or so I thought. In Mike's senior year and Joe's sophomore year, Harvard played Brown, and it was the first time they had ever been on opposite teams. Brown won, 31–19, and the sideline announcer got my boys together on camera for their reaction.

"This is the only time we've ever played against each other," Joe said. "And now that Brown has won, Mike has to live with that the rest of his life."

As friendly as they are, that sibling rivalry is always there. But just from having been around the Raiders, they both realize that their real world doesn't include pro football. Through the years, they had seen some Raider stars with no career to turn to when they were finished as players. They had seen rookies who had counted on being NFL players get cut, with no career to fall back on.

They also saw other things. Mike told me about another time he was standing with Al Davis on the sideline at training camp. Al liked to ask for opinions on players. He nudged Mike and pointed to a wide receiver who had been released by another NFL team.

"What do you think of 84?" Al asked.

"I haven't been watching him," Mike said.

"I'll give you a few minutes, just take some time and watch him, then let me know what you think." Mike focused on the wide receiver wearing 84, watched him run his patterns and catch passes. "Well," Al finally said, "what do you think?"

"He appears to be a step slow," Mike said. "He doesn't look as sharp as some of the others."

"You've got it exactly right," Al said. "He *is* a step slow. He *isn't* as sharp. And let that be a lesson to you, Michael. That's what drugs will do to you."

In another day or two, the Raiders cut the wide receiver. He drifted out of the NFL, never to return.

Watching that wide receiver moving a step slow, not as sharp as the other pass-catcher, was better than all the lectures his mother or I, or anybody else, could have given Mike and Joe about the dangers of street drugs. Their mother and I worked at raising them, but we give them credit for raising themselves.

DON'T LET A CAR DRIVE YOU

hen I'm home in California, I drive a navy blue Mercedes-Benz that Virginia gave me as a Christmas present. It's a great car, but if I had to drive a jalopy tomorrow, that would be all right too. I've always thought of a car as something that takes you places, not something that takes you to a higher status.

Even as a kid, I never went through that stage where I had to have a car. My dad was an auto mechanic at Les Vogel's Chevrolet in Daly City, so I learned at an early age that a car was just a piece of machinery with wheels, not a sex symbol. And when I got old enough to drive, my dad bought me an old, black 1940 Cadillac to drive around. It looked like a hearse.

"If something happens," he once told me, "at least you won't be in a flimsy car."

I was never in a wreck with that car, but my dad had put cars in perspective for me. You drive a car; you don't let it drive you. Then and now, I've seen kids stifled by cars, kids I grew up with, kids my own kids grew up with. I'm not even talking about serious accidents or drunk driving. I'm talking about just owning a car as a teenager. As soon as a kid owns a car, he has to pay for it. He has to get a job after school, so he no longer has the time for activities like sports or clubs. He's got to work to make the car payments and the insurance payments. So he's working after school, instead of having fun playing sports or being in the band or being on the debating team.

If the family can afford to provide a car for a teenager, that's different. Then he can still have fun, without having to worry about the finances that a car demands. But if the family can't afford it, I've always thought the kid is better off without a car.

I didn't own a car until I got married. I was coaching at Hancock Junior College when Virginia and I bought a dark blue Volkswagen bug with a convertible top. Don't laugh at the thought of me in a VW. Driving or riding, I just moved the seat back. Later on, when I was at San Diego State, we traded the VW for a brown Buick station wagon. But when I joined the Raiders, part of the deal was that I had a Dodge to drive.

If you never want to have to buy a car, be on the coaching staff of an NFL team. Every club has a local dealer who supplies the coaches with cars. As the Raiders' head coach,

I even did TV commercials for a Dodge dealer in the Oakland area. After I stopped coaching, I did TV commercials for the Toyota dealers of northern California, who provided me with a car.

Back when Virginia and I bought our VW in 1960, she was still driving a red 1957 Thunderbird convertible. But by 1964, that T-Bird needed a new something every few months—new brakes, new transmission, new tires, whatever. As much as Virginia loved that little red T-Bird, I finally convinced her that it wasn't worth the trouble anymore, and she traded it in for a Mustang. But in the years that followed, the 1957 T-Bird became a classic.

"I knew we should've kept that car," she would remind me every so often. "I just *knew* it."

I lived with that guilt for more than twenty years. Then one day, after the Hagler–Leonard fight in Las Vegas in 1987, we went to an auction of antique and classic cars at the Imperial Palace hotel, just for something to do that day. But we bought a black Volkswagen limo that Virginia drives everywhere now. And then she spotted a red 1957 T-Bird convertible.

"There it is," she said. "My car!"

Not the exact same car, but the same model, the same color, the same appeal.

"Go for it," I told her.

She kept bidding until she got it. After all those years, I finally got rid of my guilt.

YOU NEVER GET GOLF

One of my rules of life is: *never go to a restaurant where you need a reservation.* Another is: *never go to a golf course where you need a tee time.* If you need a tee time, it's too crowded for me. Too many people watching. But if you don't need a tee time, there's usually nobody out there. Or so I thought when we bought our house on the Blackhawk Country Club in the hills of Danville, California.

"Do I need a tee time?" I asked.

"Down here on the Lakeside eighteen you might need one," I was told. "But up where you live, the Falls eighteen is usually empty. From your house you can shoot out onto the ninth tee and play your way back to your house."

"Perfect."

I couldn't wait. With this house we not only had a big garage, we had every golfer's dream, a two-*cart* garage. Two golf carts, one for Virginia, one for me. The day we moved in, I strapped my golf clubs on the back of my cart, hopped in, and zoomed to the ninth tee, about fifteen seconds away. I looked around. Nobody on the tee. Nobody on the fairway. Nobody on the green.

Perfect.

The ninth hole is a slight dogleg right of only 326 yards. But it's all uphill, so it plays to about 350 yards, maybe more. Even so, it didn't look like that tough a hole if you put your drive in the fairway. That's all I wanted to do. Just put my drive in that big empty fairway from this big empty tee, then hit an iron onto that big empty green. I teed up my ball between the markers, stepped back behind the ball and looked down the fairway like I've seen Jack Nicklaus do, then walked up and settled into my stance.

Smooth, slow backswing, I reminded myself. *Good follow-through. Keep your head down.*

I waggled my driver until I was comfortable, started my backswing smoothly and slowly, and as I came through the ball, I kept my head down and followed through. But when I looked up to see where my drive was, I saw it soaring to the left.

Oh, no, I thought.

Oh, yes. I had hooked my drive out over Blackhawk Drive and it was heading toward a parked Mercedes-Benz. Its driver was standing there with his head down.

Wham! My ball thudded into the hood of his car on the fly and bounced away.

After all these years, I was finally living on a golf course where I didn't need a tee time. I finally had what amounted to my own tee, with nobody watching me. But on my very first drive off that tee, I had not only put the one person in sight on alert, the one person who probably wasn't even watching me, but I had dented the hood of his car.

Not so perfect.

But that's golf, a game like no other game. You never *get* golf. You play well one day, at least you play well for you, and you think you've got it. But you go out the next day and you haven't got it. Instead, it's got you. No matter what, you never get golf. Sooner or later, golf always gets you. Other games aren't like that. Back when I was coaching the Raiders, we could put together winning streaks. Baseball teams and basketball teams have winning streaks. But name me a golfer who's had a winning streak.

All right, Byron Nelson won eleven tournaments in a row in 1945, that's a winning streak. But that was almost half a century ago. Half a century!

For me, a winning streak in golf is two pars in a row. Believe me, I don't have a winning streak too often. I once had a thirty-nine for nine holes at Blackhawk, but usually I shoot anywhere from the low forties to the low fifties. Nine holes is enough for me. Sometimes six or seven holes. I don't know why golf is supposed to be eighteen holes. To me, golf is just a good reason to be outside doing something. After nine holes I get bored. I'm just trying to play well enough that I won't embarrass myself when I play in one-day charity tournaments.

I've been invited to play in the AT&T Pebble Beach

National Pro-Am, the one that was known as The Crosby, but I always say, "No, thank you." What I'm really saying is, "No galleries, thank you." My golf game should not be on public display at Pebble Beach.

Those one-day charity tournaments can be embarrassing enough. I even have one myself, the John Madden Charity Classic for Cal Poly at San Luis Obispo, where I played football and where I got my master's degree in education. One year I got up on the first tee and noticed a TV camera on me. I took a big swing and the ball squirted about six yards off to the left. Not even a first down. That tee shot was on the local TV news that night. But hey, it was for a good cause. Through the first five years of the tournament, we've raised about $100,000 for the Cal Poly football program. To fill the celebrity spots, I call on some of my football friends in the California area—John Robinson, Tom Flores, Jim Plunkett, Howie Long, Marcus Allen. Most of those guys have their own charity classics, so they ask me to play in their tournaments. And that's fine. But not the AT&T, not Pebble Beach, not with a big gallery. Especially not for an ex-football player like me.

Believe me, golf was not invented for people who played football. In some sports, you do things that carry over into golf. But not in football. In football, a player is taught to bend his knees, bend his arms, keep his head up, stay tense. From the time you start playing football as a little kid, you're drilled in that—knees bent, arms bent, head up, tense. All your muscles are flexed. You're ready to hit or be hit. And you never put your head down, because that's how you get hurt.

Now you go to play golf.

The first thing a golf pro tells you is to keep your head

down. There's no way a football player can keep his head down. He always had to keep his head up. He had to see what was going on. He had to see the guy he was trying to run over, or the guy who was trying to run him over. But in golf, the pro wants him to keep his head down.

Then the pro says, stand up fairly straight. There's no way a football player can stand up fairly straight. If he had stood up straight playing football, he would've been knocked down on every play.

The next thing the pro tells you is to keep your left arm straight. No way a football player can keep his left arm straight. If he had kept it straight, somebody would've snapped it in two.

Then the pro says, swing easy. Hey, no football player ever swung easy at anything or anybody. In football, it's like Lawrence Taylor says: you want to hit the quarterback so hard that snot bubbles come out of his nose. But when Lawrence Taylor plays golf, he's supposed to swing easy.

Whatever a guy has been taught to do playing football, he has to do just the opposite playing golf.

Some guys can adjust. Lawrence Taylor, I'm told, is a pretty good golfer. Mid-seventies on a good day, high seventies or low eighties the rest of the time. But not every football player can adjust. Howie Long hasn't adjusted. Howie tries to hit a golf ball as hard as he hits a quarterback. The last time I saw Howie on a golf course, he was walking off it. I was playing in the foursome behind Howie when he pushed his drive way to the right off the tenth tee at the Riviera Country Club in Los Angeles in a charity tournament. I expected to see Howie come by the ninth green, where I was waiting to putt, but Howie spun and walked toward the clubhouse.

Back when I was coaching the Raiders, our All-Pro out-side linebacker, Ted Hendricks, always talked about the Hurricane Spirit that he developed at the University of Miami.

"The Hurricane Spirit," Ted used to joke, "is very im-portant in certain situations in life. And the Hurricane Spirit is very basic: When the going gets tough, quit."

Howie Long had invoked the Hurricane Spirit and dis-appeared into the clubhouse. Which meant that in this scramble tournament, his foursome was now without its D player. In a scramble, every foursome is supposed ideally to have an A player who shoots in the seventies, a B player who shoots in the eighties, a C player who shoots in the nineties, and a D player who shoots himself. I know, I'm a D player. And from the way Howie's drive took off to the right, I knew he was a D player. But without Howie, his foursome was suddenly one guy short. So the A player in his foursome started hitting two balls on every hole. And his foursome won the tournament as a threesome. Howie even got a trophy for sitting in a clubhouse the last nine holes.

If you're the D player in a scramble, you're better off not playing. Let your A player hit two balls.

Hey, it's no fun knowing you're the D player. It's bad enough being a bad player, but it's worse when you join your group and find out you're the D player. D can stand for dumb or dense, doom or demoralized, disaster or dis-combobulated. In some scrambles, they think they're doing the D player a favor by letting him hit from the ladies' tee, but all they're doing is branding him as a D player. Every hole, he's up there on the ladies' tee with his stupid swing. And when the foursome gets to the green, the D player putts first so that he can give the good putters the line. But if he could give 'em the line, he wouldn't *be* a D player.

In some scrambles, you've got to use at least two or three drives from the D player. So now you're on the back nine and you hear, "We really need your drive on this hole." But if you could hit a good drive whenever you needed to, you wouldn't be a D player.

The day Howie Long walked off was the day I organized BUDA, the Brotherhood of United D Players of America. Hey, I *like* D players. Life is full of D players. But we needed to unite. To begin with, we shouldn't be known as D players. You get a D in school, that's bad. Call us *4* players, instead of D players. With a 4, at least we can identify with Lou Gehrig, or we can laugh it off by telling everybody we're a "Fore!" player. And if we're playing worse than usual, Howie Long will be our role model. If the going gets tough, quit. Our teams will be better off with us in the clubhouse than it would with us playing.

You'd never know it watching me swing, but I was a caddie as a kid. If you're a caddie, you're supposed to have a good swing, if only from watching good golfers swing. I've got no excuse. I used to shag balls for Ken Venturi at the San Francisco Golf Club.

When I shagged for a duffer, I had to run all over the range to pick up the balls. But with Venturi, I just stood where he told me to stand and he hit every ball so that it landed at my feet on about two bounces. He'd start with a 9-iron, then go through his bag. When he changed clubs, I'd just move back about ten yards. Same thing. Two bounces, and the ball would stop where I was standing. In grammar school, I had caddied at the Lake Merced Country Club, a dollar-fifty a bag for an eighteen-hole loop on Sunday morning. In the afternoon Lefty O'Doul, the great baseball hitter who managed the Seals and was a member at Lake Merced, would take a bunch of us kids to the Seals' game in his Cadillac convertible. Then, at Jefferson High School, I met John Gersten, Jr., whose father was the pro at the San Francisco Golf Club, just a few blocks away. John Jr. and I were on the football team together, and he talked me into being a caddie at the club where his father was the pro.

"You'll make five dollars a bag," he said.

In those years, some of the local club pros, and sometimes a touring pro, would come over every Friday afternoon to the San Francisco Golf Club to play in a gangsome. There'd be as many as twenty guys going off the first tee together. Every once in a while, Byron Nelson would show up for the gangsome. I remember his irons had skinny blades that resembled surgical instruments more than they did golf clubs. Whenever he showed up, he was the best player. And he was out there with some other good players, like Ken Venturi, who won the 1964 United States Open, and Harvie Ward, Jr., who twice won the United States Amateur.

I never got to play except on Monday, which was caddie day. I wasn't very good then, either, but nobody was very good—not even any of the old caddies like Sappho, Big Jim, and Larry. I just knew them by their first names, but the young caddies I knew from school—John Murphy, Larry Kennedy, Bob Armstrong, Bruce Owens. Those young caddies knew my name, too, but the older caddies just called me "Red." My hair is blondish now, but it was red then.

Waiting for a loop, you were always playing something. If it was really slow, you'd have time for a poker game. If you thought you might get a loop soon, you'd pitch quarters. And when all the golfers were gone, some of us would pretend we had left to go home, but then we'd sneak back onto the club grounds through a hole in the fence out near the 12th green and putt for dimes. Sometimes we putted until ten o'clock at night. Even after the sun went down, the moonlight was enough to putt by. Sometimes we all used the same putter. Sometimes we had two or three, depending on whether some of the members had given us putters they were disgusted with.

Caddies always know the holes in the fence. That's how I got into the 1955 United States Open at Olympic, just down the street from the San Francisco Golf Club.

The first day of the Open, I was ducking through the hole in the chain-link fence around Olympic when I saw a season ticket in the bushes. Someone had lost it. As a kid, I had sneaked into Kezar Stadium to see the 49ers and Seals Stadium to see the Pacific Coast League baseball games, just like I had sneaked into the Open. But now that I had found this pass, I was a legitimate spectator. I tied that pass on myself, winding the string around a belt loop so it wouldn't fall off. For the rest of the tournament I walked in the front entrance. That was a famous Open. The great Ben Hogan lost to a virtually unknown touring pro, Jack Fleck, in an eighteen-hole playoff.

I remember Fleck hit every shot really high, with a nice draw that dropped his ball into the middle of the fairway or on the green. I had nothing against Hogan, but I liked the idea of Fleck winning. It was like he'd found a hole in the fence too.

That's what I mean about golf. Jack Fleck probably thought that he had finally been able to get golf. But he didn't win another PGA Tour event for five years; then he won another tournament the following year. He had beaten Hogan head to head, but that was about it. Only three tournament victories in his career. Golf got Jack Fleck, just like it gets me and you. Hey, it even gets Jack Nicklaus, at least that's what he told me once. I was doing a CBS piece on him, and off camera, I happened to mention that as a golfer, I had no consistency. Just when I think I'm getting pretty good, I'm worse than ever.

"The same thing happens to me," Jack said. "The same thing happens to every touring pro."

It's just a matter of degree, I guess. But I also said, if he could give a recreational golfer one piece of advice, what would it be? I expected him to talk about keeping your head down or your left arm straight. Which shows how much I know.

"Play to your handicap," he said.

What Jack meant was, if you're playing a par 4, it's a par 4 for a pro, or for an amateur with a scratch handicap, but it's not a par 4 for somebody like you or me. On the front nine of the Falls course at Blackhawk, the 487-yard seventh hole is listed as a par 4. But with a big ditch in front of the green, it isn't a par 4 for me. No way can I get there in two. So what Jack meant was, I should play it as a par 5—a drive, a fairway wood or a long iron short of the ditch, a wedge to the green, and two putts. As it turned out, almost everybody at Blackhawk plays that hole as a par 5. You hear most guys say, "I can't get there in regulation," meaning two shots. But two shots isn't *our* "regulation." It's like Willie Nelson's great line about golf. Willie has his own golf course in Texas, and one day he finally putted out on a long hole for a ten.

"I parred that sucker," Willie said.

"Par?" somebody said. "You had a ten!"

"Par is ten on this hole," Willie said. "Hey, man, it's my golf course. On my golf course, this sucker is a par 10."

Willie Nelson is my kind of golfer.

Think about it. Golf is the only game where people come out once a month, sometimes once a year, and are asked to take the same "regulation" number of strokes on a hole as the touring pros do. Hey, if you play touch tackle with your kids, do you play by NFL rules? But if you play golf with your kids, you're supposed to play by "regulation" on each hole. We've got a hole at Blackhawk that's 620 yards from the tips, 605 yards from the whites. I've never seen anyone get a par 5 there. For me, it's a par 8, and that's how I play it. That's what Jack Nicklaus meant.

But when you don't even play to your personal par, that's when you want to throw a club. I never do, because I might hurt somebody, but I want to. Just like Craig Stadler wants to throw a club, but doesn't.

I like the way Craig stomps around when he's annoyed at himself. He's one of us. He jokes about how he knows how to throw a club in such a way that it'll bounce back up into his hand. Now that's a professional. If I tried to do that, I'd probably decapitate myself. With that walrus mustache and walrus body, Craig knows how to let his emotions show without overdoing it. That's not easy. People complain that too many touring pros look like clones. Blond and bland. I don't think it's fair to lump them together that way. They're out there trying to earn their living, and they're concentrating on what they're doing. If you put up gallery ropes in an accountant's office or in a farmer's barn, they might not be too exciting. But the people in the galleries and the people watching television want the golfers to be entertainers. That's asking too much of most golfers. They're trying to entertain you with their skill, like Jack Nicklaus, Arnold Palmer and Tom Watson have done throughout their careers. Most golfers are competitors, not comedians.

"True competitors," Stadler told me once. "The only money we make in a tournament is what we earn with our score."

In most other sports, you sign a contract before the season starts. If you only produce two touchdowns or only hit .200, you still get paid. If you get hurt, you still get paid. But if a golfer misses the cut in every PGA Tour event, he earns zero. If he jams his wrist hitting out of the rough and has to rest for a month, he earns zero. And nobody pays his travel expenses.

There's one thing about golf I could never understand. The older a golfer gets, the worse his putting gets. The yips, they call it. Ben Hogan had the yips. He couldn't make the short putts anymore. Putting requires the most delicate hand-eye coordination in sports. Ben lost that hand-eye coordination. But that doesn't seem to happen in other professions. The older a surgeon gets, the better he is. The older an airline pilot gets, the better he is. Or are they? Maybe we're being misled.

Golf is backwards anyway. Take a set of irons: the farther you want to hit the ball, the smaller the head of the iron. The shorter the distance, the bigger the head of the iron. If you hit down on the ball, it will go up. If you hit up on the ball, it will stay down.

In golf, everything goes by your handicap. But my real handicap is my swing, especially trying to swing with a club that's added proof that one size does not fit all. All the great golfers have been five foot nine, five-ten, and about 175 pounds, not six-four and sometimes 300 pounds. If you're my size, you've got to take this little one-size-fits-all club, hunch your shoulders, try to keep your head down and your left arm straight, then try to swing easy at a little ball. And if you try to think too much, you lose your mind.

I know, you can get longer clubs. But a longer club is harder to control. And if you're the least bit fat, you can't even see that little ball. So if you're a tall, fat, ex-football player, golf is designed to mess you up even before you swing.

Hey, the ball itself isn't that simple. I hear people talking about a hundred compression, ninety compression, the number of dimples. The way I hit the ball, sometimes I hit a red-striped range ball better than I do a new ball just out of the cellophane. But my big problem with golf balls is that I get them free. Miller Lite sends me several dozen Pinnacle balls every so often with a little Miller Lite logo on each one. That's the problem. The way I hit a golf ball, they go everywhere. Off that guy's car the first time I played the ninth hole. Up on the porch of a house across the street from the third hole. Into somebody's backyard, sometimes into a swimming pool. And whenever somebody at Blackhawk finds a ball with a little Miller Lite logo on it, they know who hit it.

"You must be John Madden," one of my neighbors said to me once. "I find those Miller Lite balls all over."

Hey, thanks a lot. Sometimes it just doesn't pay to get your golf balls free. At least not with a logo on them.

CONTRACTS AND CONSCIENCE

very so often you hear a known athlete say, "It's not in my contract to be a role model for kids." True, it's not in his contract. But if he's a decent person, it's in his conscience.

Some kids will copy whatever athletes do, for better or for worse. Just because some athletes don't want that responsibility doesn't give them the right to shirk it. Like it or not, they need to accept that responsibility of being a role model. Especially when it involves illegal drugs. Whenever a known athlete is found to have been using illegal drugs, most kids are sharp enough to know that the athlete has jeopardized his health and his career. But some kids don't see the danger. Some kids think, *Hey, if you want to be a pro athlete, you got to take drugs.* Those are the kids I worry about. And whether the known athlete likes it or not, those are the kids that *he* should be worrying about.

If the athlete wrecks his health and his career by taking drugs, that's his decision. But, unfairly, an athlete can take some kids with him.

What also bothers me is when an athlete returns from a drug rehab and plays well and some people think of him as a hero. Some kids will start thinking, *Drugs can't be so bad if you can take them and then come back from them like he did.* Those kids might experiment with drugs when they wouldn't have dared to do it before. And those kids might not be able to rehabilitate themselves.

Aside from the problem with kids, drugs have created a dilemma for teams in every sport. The team wants to eliminate drug use by its players; the team also wants to win. Sometimes there's a conflict.

Whenever a player enters drug rehab, his clubowner, general manager, and coach or manager always speak so self-righteously of how it's important to rid their team and their sport of drugs. But whenever I read that, I always wonder how long the team knew about this player's drug problem and how desperate the situation got before he entered the rehab facility. As righteous as that team might be, the club is in business to win games. To win games, a team needs all its players.

I've sometimes wondered whether a team *really* wants to help a player when it puts him in a rehab, or if it puts him away for a while in order to protect the organization from further embarrassment.

As for drug testing, each sport has a different policy. None of the policies seems to have created much fear among the athletes. The only way to create that fear is for each sport to say, "We don't allow drugs, and if you test positive, you're out. No second chance." The players would object to that. The lawyers in the various player associations would bring up "constitutional rights" and "invasion of privacy." Hey, the teams would object too. The teams wouldn't want to lose a player on one drug test.

One of the saddest commentaries on the NFL drug policy occurred in the 1986 draft of college players. At the scouting-combine camps that year, fifty-seven players were reported to have tested positive for various illegal substances. But two of those players were drafted in the very first round. Many others were drafted in the later rounds. Here were the NFL teams talking about how bad drugs were, and here were the same NFL teams drafting players with drugs on their scouting reports. Why would teams do that? Because the coach, the general manager, and maybe even the clubowner figured, *Hey, if we don't draft that player, somebody else will.*

The next year, only seven players at the scouting-combine camps were reported to have tested positive. Either that year's players were cleaner or they had cleaned up their act before the tests.

As a coach, I was lucky. I got out after the 1978 season, before the NFL's drug problem developed. Maybe I was naïve, or maybe there was a generation gap, but if any of my players were involved with cocaine, I never suspected it. I never even heard much talk about steroids. The big guys we had on the Raiders, they were naturally big guys. They didn't need steroids to get big, or bigger. But there's a difference between drugs and steroids. Drugs are a problem in our society. Steroids are a problem primarily in sports, especially football. And not just in pro football.

Steroids will develop more muscle, more bulk. With steroids, a naturally small guy can bulk up into a stronger, heavier guy.

If you know football players, you usually can tell who's a naturally big guy and who's on steroids. William Perry, The Refrigerator, The Fridge, is not on steroids. He's just not on a diet. William is a natural 300-pounder. Take it from another natural 300-pounder who's never been on steroids. I never even lifted weights that much. You can develop a bigger, stronger body by lifting weights, the way most NFL players do it. But when you look around a locker room and see a natural 195-pounder whose body now appears unnatural and out of proportion at, say, 220 pounds, he might be on steroids. That can happen at any level of football. In high school, a 170-pounder wants to be a 190-pounder. In junior college, a 190-pounder wants to be a 220-pounder. In college, a 220-pounder wants to be a 250-pounder. In the NFL, a 250-pounder wants to be a 280-pounder.

The trouble is, nobody seems to know how many steroids you should take. Even worse, nobody seems to know how damaging the aftereffects are to your heart or your kidneys or your other vital organs.

Some people don't care. Some people will do anything to succeed in sports, just like some people will do anything to succeed in business or law or medicine. Some people think that if one dose of steroids will help them, three doses will help them that much more. They don't even worry about what the consequences might be.

Athletes who use steroids also are shirking their responsibility as role models to kids. When kids see athletes bulking up as if they've been connected to the air hose at their local gas station, some will assume that steroids must be good for you. Those kids don't know the consequences.

Unfortunately, much of the publicity concerning today's athletes involves those two hazards to kids. Athletes who live normal, decent lives are written about occasionally, but not often—not nearly so often as the athletes who are busted for drugs or suspended for using steroids. As a result, most people know more about the scoundrels of sports than they do about the *real* role models.

Maybe the sense of responsibility that those scoundrels lack should be required in their contracts.

TIME OUT

In the years when I was coaching the Raiders, I'd often be sitting on our chartered bus going to our game on Sunday and staring out the window. Not really thinking about anything but the game. Not really noticing anything. Except when a car towing a boat would go by. *Hey, don't those people know this is a big game?* I always thought. *How can those people be going on their boat instead of going to the game, or at least watching it on television?* That's the way pro football coaches think—that their game is the only game in town.

But one Sunday, several years after I stopped coaching, I was driving along the Nimitz Freeway, past the Oakland Coliseum, on the way to Embarcadero Cove, where we kept our forty-seven-footer. I noticed the traffic backing up outside the Coliseum, where the Oakland Invaders were about to play a United States Football League game. *Hey*, I thought, *I'm one of those boat guys now.*

We hadn't planned to buy that forty-seven-footer. On the Fourth of July in 1979, the first Fourth of July since I was a little kid when I wasn't thinking about the football season coming up, our friends Hank and Rita Torian invited Virginia, our boys, and me out on their fifty-footer, a Grand Banks cruiser with all the toys on it. We went out on San Francisco Bay, up into San Pablo Bay, over to the delta of the Sacramento River, and then back down through San Francisco Bay just as the sun was setting behind the Golden Gate Bridge.

"This is great," Mike said.

"It's really fun," agreed Joe.

"I could get to like this," Virginia said. "Maybe we ought to think about getting a boat someday."

"Yeah," I said. "Someday."

Several days later, Virginia went to a hospital to visit Kay Shaw, who had taught sixth grade in Pleasanton at the same time she did. Kay was dying of lung cancer. In their conversation that day, Virginia talked about having spent the Fourth of July on the Torian boat.

"It was beautiful," Virginia said. "We're thinking about getting a boat someday."

"Don't wait for someday," Kay said. "Someday might never come. Do it now."

The next weekend, we went up to the delta to look at boats. We liked one, but then we saw another boat that was a little longer, and we liked that better. Then we saw another one that was a little longer still, and we liked that even more.

"Every time you see one that's a foot longer," Mike said, "that's the one you want."

As it turned out, we decided a forty-seven-foot C. and L. Trawler was long enough. Pat O'Daniels, the production manager of *Bay and Delta Yachtsmen* magazine, later had a contest to name the boat. The winning entry was *Time Out,* the perfect name for a retired football coach's boat. The only trouble was, none of us knew how to drive the boat. At first we just sat in the boat at the dock. After a couple of weekends of that, I decided to hire a guy to take us out on the water. Then I thought, *This is stupid; the next time he can teach us how to drive it.* But when he tried to teach me, he discovered what I've known all my life and what Virginia learned the hard way: I'm a mechanical moron.

"You turn it with the engines," he kept telling me.

I couldn't get the hang of it at all. Joe was too young then, but Virginia and Mike got to the point where each could handle it pretty well. Then one day Virginia slammed it into a slip.

"That's it," she yelled. "Mike, you're the captain now."

Mike took us everywhere. We never went past the Golden Gate, but there was no need to go out there. From the southern end of San Francisco Bay to San Pablo Bay, and over through the delta, we had more than a thousand miles of waterways to explore. In an hour's cruise, you can sometimes get as much as a 50-degree variance in temperature. If it was cold, we went up near the delta, where it was warmer. And if we were warm, we went over near San Francisco, where it was cooler. Anytime we were out in the breeze coming through the Golden Gate, we were cool, if not cold. When we wanted to get warm, we went over to Cimarron or Sausalito or Angel Island, anyplace that was sheltered from that breeze coming through the Golden Gate from the Pacific Ocean.

"Today," Mike used to joke, "I think we'll go wherever I want to go, because I'm the only one who can drive this boat."

That was fine, when Mike was around. But when he went off to prep school at Choate, and then to Harvard, we had a boat without a captain. We went back to just sitting on it. Then we put it up for sale. After about four years, somebody finally bought it.

"Happiest day of my life," Virginia said.

STUDENTS AND ATHLETES

No matter how many college sports scandals occur, no matter how many NCAA investigations develop, no matter how many college presidents and college athletic officials and coaches insist that it won't happen again, it happens again. And again. It happens because college sports is big business. It happens because some college athletes are expected to be college students.

But just because a teenager appears to be a physical genius at football or basketball, that doesn't mean that he's a mental genius in the classroom. As soon as a kid scores twenty touchdowns for his high-school football team, or averages twenty-seven points a game in basketball, everybody wants to know where he's going to college. With some kids, that's an unfair question. Academically, they're simply not college material. They'll never be real student-athletes.

According to the NCAA, in order for an incoming freshman to be eligible for varsity sports, he or she must have a 2.0 grade point average in an eleven-course core high school curriculum, as well as a combined score of 700 on the SAT exams. Once a freshman qualifies for admission, academic eligibility varies from college to college, from conference to conference.

I don't pretend to have all the answers to this question, but I've always thought that every college should have two types of programs: its regular program, which leads to an academic degree, and another program with specialized courses in certain subjects that lead to an associate degree or a certificate.

Back when I was the football coach at Hancock Junior College, in Santa Maria, California, I was on the curriculum committee. We had one curriculum for students who intended to transfer their credits to a four-year college, and another curriculum for students who wanted to take courses in a certain subject but not transfer the credits. What we did was acknowledge that everyone who went to junior college wasn't necessarily college-degree material.

I think a similar system would work in four-year colleges. It wouldn't involve just athletes; it would be for people who wanted to be artists, or musicians, people with a talent they wanted to develop without having to take other courses that didn't interest them.

Hey, that wouldn't stop college athletic programs from cheating. They could put all their football players in an art class, or all their basketball players in a music class, and never take attendance. Just tell the professor to give the athletes a B, and that's it. No, the kids would have to go to class, they would have to take exams, they would be required to make progress in their particular subject toward an associate degree or a certificate. But they wouldn't be thrown into an academic situation that was way over their heads.

The trouble in college sports is not merely the under-the-table payments and the academic hoodwinking. The basic hypocrisy is maintaining that every teenage athlete who enters college is potentially a college graduate. By acknowledging that's not so, the colleges would put the situation out in the open.

Another solution for college sports would be for the NFL to create minor leagues in football and the NBA to create them in basketball.

As it is now, the NFL and the NBA use the colleges as their farm systems. Major league baseball uses its minor leagues *and* college baseball as a farm system. Maybe that's the reason that you seldom hear about academic scandals in college baseball. If a kid wants to go to college to play baseball, chances are he's college material. If a kid prefers to enter a team's farm system after high school, chances are he's not college material.

If pro football and pro basketball had minor leagues, that wouldn't stop kids who aren't college material from going to college, but it *would* provide a choice for the kid who isn't college material.

Some years ago I talked to Bobby Knight, the Indiana University basketball coach, about the minor league theory in football and basketball. He believes it would benefit both the colleges and the athletes. The colleges would no longer be forced to recruit a kid who wouldn't ever think of going to college if he was not a good athlete. And the athletes wouldn't be trapped into having to go to college in order to put themselves on athletic display for the NFL and the NBA.

"I wouldn't mind recruiting against the Boston Celtics," Bobby said. "I'd still get the kid who wanted to go to college, and the Celtics would get the kid who wanted to play minor league basketball."

In pro basketball, two or three NBA teams could sponsor a minor league franchise in a league with, say, ten teams. In pro football, two NFL teams could sponsor a minor league franchise in a league with fourteen teams. If the NBA and the NFL worked at the idea, it could be a success. And it would solve many of the problems that infiltrate college sports.

The curriculum plan puts the onus on the colleges. The minor league plan puts the onus on the NFL and the NBA. Either way, the onus would be off the athlete who isn't college material.

TWO LUMPS
OF SUGAR

T he morning after Sugar Ray Leonard snatched the world middleweight title from Marvelous Marvin Hagler, I was walking through Caesars Palace on the way back to my room from breakfast. Near the Olympic lounge, not far from the big, gray marble statue of Joe Louis, a guy in a sweat suit tapped me on the shoulder.

"Ray would like to see you," he said. "He's right here in the lounge."

The lounge was all but empty. Two or three people were at the bar. At a table in the back, Sugar Ray and his son, Ray Jr., were looking up at a TV set that was carrying a replay of the closed-circuit video tape. I walked over, shook hands with Ray and his son, and sat down. Up on the screen just then, Ray stuck out his face and glared, as if daring Hagler to punch him, then darted away. Sitting there, Ray smiled.

"I don't remember doing that," he said.

The more Ray watched, the more he saw things that he didn't remember. Throwing quick combinations, then darting away. Being cornered, then fighting his way off the ropes. "I don't remember that," he kept saying. "I don't remember that at all." He seemed to be seeing the fight for the first time, as if he had never been in that ring. Or he seemed to be watching another boxer instead of himself. But he remembered some things. Like how tired he was when he wobbled to his corner after the tenth round.

"I didn't think I could make it the last two rounds," he said. "I thought I was going to die."

During both the eleventh and twelfth rounds, Ray would clinch, then peek over Marvin's shoulder toward his corner, where Angelo Dundee, Janks Morton, and Dave Jacobs were hunched down below the steps.

"I was asking them to let me know when there was one minute left," he said. "For one minute, I knew I could do anything."

When the bell ended the twelfth round, Ray jumped up and down, celebrating what he (correctly) assumed to be his victory by a decision—a split decision, as it turned out. Then just as quickly, he sagged to the canvas in exhaustion.

"I don't remember that, either," he said. "I think the fight drained my memory as well as my body."

Sitting there in the lounge, Ray was still drained. He spoke slowly, quietly. His body sagged like a balloon after all its air has escaped. But he knew how he had won.

"When Marvin started calling me names," Ray said, "I knew he was frustrated. I knew I had him."

Ray Leonard's victory was not only one of the great feats in boxing history, but also one of the great feats in *sports* history. Except for a ninth-round knockout of Kevin Howard in 1984, he hadn't had a fight in more than five years. He had needed surgery in 1982 to repair a detached retina in his left eye. And he hadn't even had a tune-up to see how his reflexes were, to see how his eye had held up. After that layoff, he was challenging an undisputed middleweight champion who had reigned since 1980, who hadn't lost a fight in nearly eleven years, who had a 62–2–2 record.

But somehow, Ray Leonard won. If he had won after a layoff of a year, or even two years, it would have been remarkable enough. His winning after a virtual five-year layoff was almost incredible.

I can't imagine any other athlete in any other sport doing what Ray Leonard did after a five-year layoff. O. J. Simpson couldn't rush for one hundred yards against NFL defenses. Willie Brown couldn't shut out an NFL wide receiver. Reggie Jackson couldn't hit a home run off a major-league fastball. Fernando Valenzuela couldn't strike out ten batters with a major-league screwball. Larry Bird or Magic Johnson couldn't score thirty points in an NBA playoff game. Even if those guys *tried* to do that, none of them would possess the same quickness and instincts as they had at the peak of their careers. And yet Ray Leonard showed the same quickness and instincts against Marvelous Marvin Hagler as he had against

Thomas Hearns in 1981, and against Roberto Duran in 1980.

Aside from football, boxing has always been my favorite sport. My dad and my grandpa were fight fans. My grandpa lived with us, and he couldn't hear too well, so he would put his ear right next to our big wooden box-radio when Don Dunphy was doing the blow-by-blow on the Friday night fights. Those fights started at ten o'clock in the east, which meant seven o'clock in Daly City, where we lived. After dinner I would sit with my dad and my grandpa and listen. One of my first memories is of hearing Joe Louis knock out Billy Conn in the thirteenth round of their 1941 heavyweight title fight.

"Sooner or later," I remember my dad saying, "I knew Louis would get him."

In those years before television, listening to the Friday night fights was our big link to eastern sports. At that time, remember, there were no NFL teams in California, no major league baseball teams, no NBA teams. All we had was college sports, minor league baseball, and an occasional big fight. The first big fight I ever *saw* was Sugar Ray Robinson's fifteen-round decision over Carl (Bobo) Olson at the Cow Palace in San Francisco in 1952, about six months after he had knocked out Randy Turpin to regain the middleweight title.

As good as seeing the fight was, seeing Sugar Ray Robinson train in Newman's gym, downtown, was even better. Newman's gym was old and smelly, with old guys sitting around smoking cigars. But when Sugar Ray trained there that day, he turned it into a fancy theater. He punched the bag to music. Instead of skipping rope, he just slapped the rope on the floor, again to music. To this day, I think Sugar Ray Robinson was the greatest athlete I've ever seen in person. The things he did with his hands, his feet, his whole body, were just amazing.

"This guy's terrific," I remember my pal John Robinson saying that day in Newman's gym. "We've got to see this fight."

So the night Sugar Ray fought at the Cow Palace, we sneaked in. And as much as I enjoyed seeing Sugar Ray, my pal John enjoyed it even more. He even tried to tell everybody that his first name was really Ray.

"I'm Ray Robinson," he'd say, shadowboxing on the street. "I'm Ray Robinson."

Except for some televised fights, I didn't see Sugar Ray Robinson again until the 1984 Summer Olympics in Los Angeles. I was there doing radio spots for RKO, and I always stopped at the boxing tournament. One night when I was sitting with Charley Steiner of RKO, the crowd started buzzing.

"Somebody big is coming in," I said.

Sugar Ray Robinson, as silky smooth as ever, had arrived. Mark Breland, who would win the Olympic lightweight gold medal, won by a knockout that night, and afterward I went back to the interview area. Over in a corner, Sugar Ray was sitting by himself. In a few minutes, Breland arrived and sat behind a table on a small platform. Some young boxers like to pretend they're Muhammad Ali, bragging and spouting. But not Breland.

"When I looked down from my corner and saw Sugar Ray Robinson," he said, "I thought, 'I've got to make this my best fight of the tournament.' I hope it was. I know I can never be compared to Mr. Robinson, but just to fight in front of him was a thrill. And now that I see him here, I'd like to introduce him."

When Sugar Ray stood up, he was glowing. That's my

fondest memory of the Olympics, listening to Mark Breland talk about Sugar Ray Robinson and then watching Sugar Ray glow. And that's one of the best things about boxing, being able to hang out with the boxers, especially before a big fight. Ever since I stopped coaching, I've had the time to go to Las Vegas and Atlantic City for some of the big fights. Those days before a big fight are the best hangout I know. Watching one fighter train, then watching the other fighter train. Sitting around talking about how you think the fight will go. And even better, listening to other people talk about how they think the fight will go.

I don't try to be a boxing expert. I'm just a fan. But boxing is so basic, so subjective, that somebody who just landed here from another planet has as valid an opinion on a big fight as somebody who's been around boxing all his life.

Boxing isn't like other sports. In football, if you blitz eight players, the other team won't be able to protect their quarterback. In baseball, if the pitcher can't get the ball over the plate, you walk. In basketball, if you work the backdoor play correctly, it's two points. But in boxing, there's no blitz, no backdoor play, no base on balls. There's just two guys with gloves.

Who do you like? Will it be a knockout? Or will it be a decision? If it's a knockout, which round?

When the bell rings, all those opinions don't do either guy any good. For sheer action, the best fight I've ever seen was Marvelous Marvin Hagler's third-round knockout of Thomas Hearns, at Caesars Palace in 1985. In those eight minutes, I never took my eyes off the two fighters. Not even between rounds. Usually, in the first round, you settle into your seat, you observe how the two fighters are feeling each other out, you talk to the guy next to you about how the fight is shaping up. But at that fight, I never even settled into my seat.

In the third round, Hagler's forehead started to bleed. When the referee took him over to the ropes for the doctor to look at his cuts, I thought, *Uh-oh, it must be serious, maybe the doctor will stop the fight.* But then I happened to look back at Hearns, and his legs were quivering. His legs were gone. When the doctor let Hagler continue, I knew it was only a matter of time. And it was.

That's why I thought Marvin would be just too much for Sugar Ray Leonard, too much fury, too much hunger. I'd always been fascinated about why it's so hard for a Super Bowl or World Series championship team to repeat the following year. But here was a boxer who had reigned as the middleweight champion for more than six years, a boxer who hadn't lost in eleven years. And when I watched him train in Palm Springs, before the Hearns fight, I understood why. For all the millions he had made, he was still hungry to win.

Most champions like to be surrounded by an entourage. When Marvin showed up for his workout, he was carrying his own equipment bag. The only people with him were his co-managers the Petronelli brothers, Pat and Goody (who's also his trainer), and his sparring partners.

In his own way, Marvin was making sure he was still hungry. It's not easy. If you're not hungry, how do you make yourself hungry? If you've got a fridge full of food, how can you say you're hungry? But he did it. Here he was, training among the palm trees at the Americana Canyon resort in Palm Springs but as soon as he entered that tent for his workout, he reverted to being the Marvin Hagler who grew up with the Newark race riots, who moved to Brockton, Massachusetts, where he worked on construction gangs, who had to struggle for so many years early in his boxing career.

I thought Marvin was going to handle Ray Leonard, not easily but decisively. Maybe in a middle-round knockout. But when it didn't turn out that way, most people in boxing owed Ray an apology.

Nobody seemed to understand why Ray Leonard was making a comeback just to fight Marvin after a virtual five-year layoff. But all those people who were criticizing him for risking a comeback could never understand why Ray got into the ring as a kid. If you don't have the mentality to be a fighter in the first place, you certainly don't have the mentality to understand why somebody would want to fight again, to understand why Ray believed that he wasn't going to get hurt. Ray was thinking about how he was going to win, not how he was going to get hurt.

Whenever there's a boxing death, some sports columnists and TV commentators demand that boxing be abolished. I don't think boxing should be abolished, just like I don't think football is too violent. But that doesn't mean that I believe boxing, or football, or any other sport, should ignore ways to make it safer.

Occasionally a boxer dies. Some eventually suffer brain damage. But nobody forced them to be boxers. They *wanted* to be boxers, in hopes of making big money, or being famous, or maybe just because they liked to fight. And no boxer ever made big money without earning it, without having trained and worked and struggled for years. As soon as Ray Leonard announced his comeback, most people talked about how he didn't need the money, how he was jeopardizing the sight in his left eye. But those people didn't understand that Ray was coming back for the same reason he got into boxing as a kid. He liked to fight.

That's the way boxers think. That's why they make comebacks. That's why they hang on longer than they should, like Muhammad Ali did.

Coaching the Raiders and working for CBS kept me from going to any of Ali's fights except one, his 1972 seventh-round knockout of Jerry Quarry in Las Vegas when Virginia and I were there on vacation. Ali wasn't the heavyweight champion then, but he was still the best show in sports. In or out of the ring. I remember him on a TV talk show, where he was cracking jokes about hurricanes.

"They're bad, they knock down homes, they flood towns," he said. Then he laughed. "But what do you expect of *hurri*canes? Think about that. They don't call them *hissi*canes. They call them *hurri*canes."

As sharp as Ali was, he fought too long. His doctors don't link his Parkinson's syndrome to boxing, but he still fought too long. That's the boxing mentality, especially for somebody who was as great a champion as Ali was. Ali came back in 1980 to challenge Larry Holmes, but even when he looked terrible, he didn't believe he was. When he hardly won a round in losing a ten-round decision to Trevor Berbick in the Bahamas in 1981, he was finally convinced that he shouldn't fight anymore.

After all those years of admiring Ali, I finally got to see him introduced at the Thomas Hearns–Roberto Duran super welterweight title fight in 1984 at Caesars Palace. Afterward, my son Mike heard that Ali was across the street in The Dunes, so Mike and his friends went over to see him. Ali shook hands with them, stood for a snapshot, signed autographs and then talked to them for fifteen minutes. About everything and anything. Mike was thrilled.

One of my regrets is that I never had the opportunity to hang out with boxing people before one of Ali's big fights. I didn't realize the fun of a boxing hangout until I went to the Larry Holmes–Gerry Cooney heavyweight title fight at Caesars Palace in 1982 to do RKO radio spots. On one of my first days there, Gerry invited me up to his suite.

"Have dinner with us," he said. "Then we'll play poker."

My kind of night. The dinner was good. The poker was good. And the conversation was good. We talked football. We talked movies. And the more we talked, the more I realized that nobody was talking about the fight. Nobody was talking about how Gerry should attack Larry Holmes, or where Larry was vulnerable. I thought, *This is strange; the week of a Raider game, all we talked about was how to beat the other team, but hey, maybe this is how they do it in boxing.*

If that's how they did it in boxing, it didn't work for Gerry Cooney. He got stopped in the thirteenth round. Then he all but disappeared until 1987, when he fought Michael Spinks in Atlantic City. The day of that fight, I was in the elevator at the Trump Plaza on the way up to my room, when Rich Rose got on. Rich was handling Gerry's publicity.

"You want to say hello to Gerry?" Rich asked. "Follow me."

Gerry's room, it turned out, was right next to my room. We talked about football, about my new bus. We watched Vanna White turn the letters on *Wheel of Fortune*, and Gerry was the first one to put the letters together. But just like five years earlier, nobody talked about the fight. The only time Gerry even referred to it was when somebody mentioned the weigh-in.

"They must've fixed the scales so Spinks would look heavier," Gerry said. "I know I weighed 234, but the scale had me at 238."

Whatever his weight was, Gerry was awful. He got knocked out in the fifth round. There must be nothing worse for a boxer than the hours after he's lost a fight, especially if he's been knocked out. He must feel like he's all alone in the world. When I went up to my room, I glanced at the door of his room. If it had been open or even ajar, I would've knocked and tried to console him. But his door was closed. I just went to my room. The more I thought about what Gerry Cooney was unable to accomplish that night, after a virtual five-year layoff, the more I appreciated what Sugar Ray Leonard had accomplished. And the more I came to believe that boxing is the toughest sport of all.

The way to tell the toughest sport is by how long athletes need to rest before their next appearance. They play baseball every day. They play golf and tennis almost every day. They play basketball and hockey three or four times a week. They play football once a week. But a boxer usually needs a few weeks to recuperate, and then he doesn't fight again for another few weeks, sometimes for another few months. I guess marathon runners need more than a week to recuperate, but nobody's hitting them when they're running. That's why boxing is, to me, the toughest sport of all. But that doesn't mean a boxer is a better athlete than, say, a marathon runner or any other athlete. Deciding who the best athlete is depends on whose arena you're in.

I think Rick Barry will attest to that.

One day when I was the Raiders' coach, Rick Barry of the Golden State Warriors visited our training camp. At the time, Rick was one of the NBA's best forwards. At six feet seven, he could shoot, he could pass, he could rebound, he could run. He was a four-time NBA first-team All Star, a four-time ABA first-team All Star, and now he's in the Basketball Hall of Fame. He was also a good tennis player and a good golfer. But he believed that, as a group, pro basketball players were the world's best athletes. At our training camp, he wanted to put on a Raider uniform to show what a superb athlete he was.

"Hi, coach," he said. "I'm just going to run some patterns."

I go along with a gag as well as anybody, but not when it comes to my business. At the time, pro football was my business.

"Yeah, you can run some patterns," I said, "but this is a live drill. We're shooting live bullets out there in this drill."

Our two safeties, Jack Tatum and George Atkinson, happened to walk by. I introduced Rick to Jack and George, then I had a word with Jack, one of the NFL's hardest-hitting defensive backs. "Rick's going to be running some patterns," I said, "but if he comes inside and catches the ball, don't take it easy on him just because he's a basketball player. We're not giving him any deals here."

Rick looked at Jack and George, then he looked at me. He smiled, nodded, turned, and walked away.

Rick didn't want any part of the football arena, and I didn't blame him. But that's what I mean about who the best athlete is depending on whose arena you're in. If you put Jack Tatum and George Atkinson, or any other football players, in the basketball arena, Rick Barry would be the better athlete. If you put Rick Barry in the football arena, Jack Tatum and George Atkinson and the other football players would be the better athletes. And Rick knew it.

But the arguments will always go on. Who's the best athlete? What's the toughest sport?

At a Miller Lite commercial a few years ago, the one where Bob Uecker goes underwater to hit a golf ball, I decided to stir up the guys by asking what they thought was the toughest sport. Their answers were predictable. The baseball guys insisted that trying to hit a curveball and playing every day was tougher than anything else. The basketball guys stuck up for basketball. The football guys stuck up for football. The hockey guys stuck up for hockey. Whatever their sport was, they stuck up for it. When it was my turn, I pointed to Alexis Arguello, once the world lightweight, super featherweight, and featherweight champion.

"That guy's sport is the toughest sport," I said. "Boxing is the toughest sport."

"No, no," Bob Uecker said. "The toughest sport is bullfighting. You're out there with a big red napkin, that's all, and that bull is trying to stick his horns in your guts. *That's* the toughest sport."

Nobody else knew what to say, but Alexis Arguello nodded. "He's right," Alexis said. "That's tougher than boxing."

MY SHOELACE VOW

s a little kid, I always hated to get dressed up. I still do. About the only time I even look dressed up is when I'm in the CBS booth doing an NFL game. On camera I have to wear my blue blazer over a shirt and tie. But what's not on camera are my sneakers with their laces flopping. Years ago, I vowed to myself that if I ever got to where I didn't have to tie my shoes, I never would. I haven't tied my shoes in maybe ten years. Even when I do get dressed up, I wear loafers. I hate what I call hard shoes.

I own two suits, a blue suit and a gray suit. I've even got

a tuxedo, but that's another chapter. Other than that, my only suits are sweat suits. I've got a few sports jackets, and some nice slacks, but I seldom wear them. With my size, I've never felt that I look good, no matter how good the clothes are. There's no point putting whipped cream on manure.

If I have to wear a suit, I do. I'm not trying to project an image as an oddball. I know when I should get dressed up. Before the Michael Spinks–Gerry Cooney heavy-weight fight in Atlantic City in 1987, I was invited to a party Donald Trump had at his Trump Plaza hotel. I wore my gray suit, a white shirt with a dark blue tie, blue socks and black loafers. But when I'm just hanging out some-where, I'll be wearing sweatpants and a sport shirt.

I'm sure this all goes back to when I was a little kid who hated to get dressed up to be around adults. Or to get dressed up to go to church, even for my first communion or my confirmation. I hated a tie around my neck.

In my early years as the Raiders' coach, I wore a tie on the sideline, but the tie was always loose, never tight up there around the collar. Some people used to wonder how I could walk around the sideline in cold weather in my shirtsleeves, but believe me, I didn't feel cold. My adrena-line kept me warm. So did my involvement in the game. I never had time to think about being cold. When it was real cold, as it always was in Pittsburgh in the playoffs, I wore a warm jacket. But as soon as the game ended, I couldn't wait to take it off.

That also goes back to when I was a little kid. If it was cool or rainy in Daly City, my mother always made me put on a hat, and a sweater or a jacket, when I went off to school in the morning. But as soon as I got up the block, I'd take them off.

I was lucky. As a kid, I never had to wear a tie in grammar school or high school. And when I went to Cal Poly in San Luis Obispo, there were no girls there, so none of the guys bothered to dress up. I've always thought that most people dress for the opposite sex. But with no opposite sex around, nobody dressed. When you got up, you just threw on whatever happened to be handy. That's when I started walking around in sneakers with the laces flopping. And when I started coaching, that's when I vowed that if I ever got to where I didn't have to tie my shoes, I never would.

I used to buy clothes at those Big Man's stores. But because of all the commercials I do, I hardly have to buy clothes anymore. Whenever I'm going to do a commercial, somebody from the advertising agency will phone and say, "This is the wardrobe we'd like you to bring." But then I say, "I don't have that in my wardrobe. You know me, I'm a sweat suit guy." They don't know what to say to that, except to ask what size jacket and slacks I wear.

"I wear a fifty-two long jacket," I'll say.

The waist size on the slacks will vary, depending on whether I've been on a diet or not. And when I show up to do the commercial, the ad agency has supplied the wardrobe they want me to wear. When the commercial is done, they don't know what to do with the clothes.

"You might as well keep the clothes," somebody always says.

By now, some of the best clothes in my closet are from commercials. Nice clothes. But on me, they're just whipped cream for manure.

FORKS IN
MY TUX

Outside, my name was in lights, which made me uncomfortable to begin with. The sign on the marquee at Del Webb's High Sierra casino-hotel in Lake Tahoe, Nevada, read, "Welcome John Madden's 50th Birthday Roast and Super Bowl XI Champions." And inside, up on the dais, I was even more uncomfortable. I was wearing a tuxedo. My own, not a rented one.

Several years earlier I had rented the same tux, a 52 long, when I had to go to a big dinner. But when I realized that I might as well own one, I bought it. The way I usually dress, in sweat suits and sneakers, my tux is a family joke. At home there's a color snapshot of me in it, looking straight ahead and smiling. On it, our son Mike has written, "You rang, Mrs. Madden?" And on March 28, 1987, here I was wearing my tux in the High Sierra Theatre for the Super Bowl XI reunion and roast that my friend Parris Farzar had organized. Parris is the director of customer relations for Del Webb Hotels, and we've known each other for about twenty years.

"Let's have a roast," Parris said one day.

"I don't want to be roasted," I said. "I've already been roasted. After I stopped coaching, remember? I've been through that drill."

"Let's have a birthday party."

"I don't want a birthday party. I don't really want to do anything for my fiftieth birthday."

"Let's have a reunion."

"What kind of reunion?"

"It'll be the tenth anniversary of Super Bowl XI; let's have a reunion of your Super Bowl team."

"Now you're talking."

This way, it wasn't just for me. It was for the guys on that Super Bowl team, and it was also for charity. I'd always thought about establishing a John Madden Foundation, for kids who don't really have a chance to do much with their lives, for either mental or physical reasons. This reunion of the Super Bowl XI team seemed like the perfect way to raise some money. As it turned out, we cleared about $75,000 to get the foundation going. But the big problem wasn't selling the tickets. The big problem was finding some of the players.

"Otis Sistrunk," Parris said to me. "Nobody knows where Otis is."

Otis was one of our defensive tackles on that Super Bowl team, the big bald guy who had never gone to college. In the ABC booth during one of our Monday night games, Alex Karras noticed the steam coming off Otis's shaved head.

"Otis," said Alex, "must be from the University of Mars."

For all we knew, Otis had returned to Mars, but after about ten phone calls, Parris finally tracked him down in North Carolina somewhere. Otis had arrived for the reunion, along with about two dozen other members of our Super Bowl XI championship team. The only starters who didn't show were Fred Biletnikoff, the wide receiver who was chosen as the most valuable player in that Super Bowl game, our fullback Pete Banaszak, and Willie Hall, one of our inside linebackers. They had other commitments. That was too bad, because they would have enjoyed the reunion as much as everybody else did—and a lot more than any of us enjoyed getting ready for that Super Bowl game.

"You're going to get more publicity than you ever got in your life," I remember telling my players before that Super Bowl. "Enjoy it."

I think they tried to enjoy it. I tried to. But we couldn't enjoy it completely. Hanging over us was the pressure of the game, the pressure to win. There's no way you can enjoy it completely until you win the game. By then, winning is more of a relief than anything else. It's too late to enjoy all the days leading up to the game. Ten years later, it's different. It's like kids in high school or college; they don't realize how much they're enjoying it. Then they go back ten years later and say, "Didn't we have fun?" It was the same way with our Super Bowl team.

Most of the guys arrived Friday night, but we didn't all get together until Saturday at a brunch. Each of the guys got up and talked, then Mike Ornstein of the Raiders' front office announced that some Super Bowl XI posters were available for anybody who wanted one.

If I had offered my players a poster ten years earlier, during Super Bowl week, nobody would have bothered taking one. Or if somebody did take one, he would've written something stupid on it, or folded it into a paper airplane. But now, all these guys rushed up to get a poster. The next thing I knew, each one was getting his teammates to autograph it. Ten years later, they were finally enjoying what they had accomplished. And when the roast began, they seemed to enjoy it even more. After the Super Bowl XI film was shown, Joey Bishop, the master of ceremonies, introduced Gene Upshaw, the Hall of Fame left guard and offensive captain on that team, now the executive director of the NFL Players Association.

"It's a privilege," Gene began, "to be on such an honored dais with so many good friends, and see that life has treated some of them very well. And in some cases, too well," he said, glancing at me. "Look at the size of this man. When we were preparing for this Super Bowl, we knew we were going to win the game. There was no doubt in our minds that we'd win. But around the locker room, there was a lot of talk about who was going to carry Madden off the field. That was really the most important thing at the Super Bowl. That's why it took so long for us to win. We had to go out and find guys like John Matuszak and Charles Philyaw, people who could actually pick this man up. That week I looked at Art Shell and I said, 'Art, you want to help carry John off the field?' He said, 'No, I'll hurt my back!'

"You saw the film where John was being carried off the field. Well, if they ran that film a little longer, you would've noticed that they dropped him. They did not make it. They actually dropped him. No one could possibly carry this man."

Out in the audience, more than 850 people were laughing, but then Gene went on, "On behalf of the players that are here and the players that had an opportunity to work under your leadership, you had a tremendous effect on our lives. And whatever we do, you'll always be a part of it." Nice words, and I appreciated them, but at a roast, the roastee doesn't speak until all the roasters have stuck a fork in him. Larry Csonka was next. Big Zonk had been a Hall of Fame fullback for the Miami Dolphins, but now he was wearing his Miller Lite blue blazer.

"I guess I have to convey Coach Shula's apologies for not being here tonight," Zonk said. "His wife is very ill, and he called me and asked if I would come down here and make an official statement on his behalf, which I'm doing. Now you have the official statement.

"My personal opinion is that Coach Shula is not here because he doesn't like you, John. You want to know the truth, I don't like you either. If you took a poll of all the guys on this podium, probably ninety-five percent of 'em don't like John either," he said, glancing down the dais at Ken Stabler, who with his long white hair looked like an old Confederate general who had just gotten off his horse. "Snake down there *thinks* he likes John, but he doesn't know about the deal John struck with the devil, where John stays young and Snake doesn't.

"John's an interesting guy, all right. One time he hollered something really nasty at me about my heritage. I looked flabbergasted. I said, 'John, I've looked up to you like an older brother, like a father image. I can't believe you said something like that to me.'

"Being a fast thinker, John walked over and put his arm around me, and said, 'Zonk, you're right, I was a little off-color there. I apologize. We have to look beyond our relationship and beyond these two teams. We have to look at the overall good of football. What I'd like you to do is fumble the ball.'

"John's that kind of guy. He's got that kind of warm heart. You can tell by all these people up here that we're all for him. His co-announcer's here, isn't he?"

Zonk looked around, but Pat Summerall wasn't there. Pat was working the Tournament Players Championship golf tournament that weekend. Barry Frank wasn't there either. Barry is the president of Transworld International, the television wing of the International Management Group that Mark McCormack founded. Barry had sent a video tape of an imaginary telephone conversation with me that was now up on the screen.

"Your book sale is terrific," Barry was saying on the tape. "It's more than McCormack's book. No, not as much as the Bible yet. But a few more weeks on the best-seller list and you'll catch the Bible, no question."

When that tape ended, Joey Bishop announced that another tape would now be shown. "Again," he explained, "it's a couple of men who unfortunately could not make it here, but this was really a beautiful moment. How they rehearsed and prepared for this was beautiful." When the tape came on, Pat Summerall didn't say a word, he just stared straight ahead. "They rehearsed this," Joey said, "a week and a half." Then Jimmy (The Greek) Snyder was seen staring blankly, not saying a word.

"There it is, John," Joey said. "Two men who love you."

Joey then introduced somebody who *was* there: Mike Ditka, the Chicago Bears' coach. "John is probably the picture of success," Mike began. "You stop and think what he's accomplished as a coach. Winning more than a hundred games in ten years is unbelievable, truly a great accomplishment, besides the Super Bowl. He's gone into television, he's become the best-known analyst and probably the *best* analyst in the game. He's also very famous for his commercials. This is a picture of success, and the thing that makes me so happy, and makes me know that this is the right kind of guy, is that John has never let that success go to his clothes.

"I've seen John on numerous occasions, but tonight's the first time I've ever seen him in anything but tennis shoes."

Next was Jim Tunney, the NFL official who was the referee in Super Bowl XI, when we beat the Minnesota Vikings, 32–14.

"John, you look great," Jim said. "You're finally wearing my colors. Black and white. And yes, I refereed that Super Bowl game. But in August of 1977, seven months later, the Kingdome, the Oakland Raiders are playing a pre-season game against the Seattle Seahawks, who were then in their second year. Before the game John was walking around the field, and I had my son Mark with me, about sixteen at the time. I introduced him to Coach Madden, and I looked down and saw this magnificent Super Bowl ring. I said, 'John, I don't understand. You were the coach of the Oakland Raiders in Super Bowl XI, I was the referee. You were on the field the same time I was, three hours. We prepared working at our own jobs. How come you've got this magnificent ring and the league gives me this crummy watch?' John says, without hesitation, 'Because you don't care who wins.'

"John Madden cared about winning. John Madden developed and prepared to win. The greatest thing about a winner is, John Madden won. It's nice to be with a winner."

Tom Flores, Kenny Stabler, Dave Rowe, and Monte Clark also zinged me, then Joey Bishop introduced the man who would introduce the members of our Super Bowl team. "Ladies and gentlemen," Joey said, "I leave you with two very talented words . . . Al Davis." My old boss, the Raiders' managing general partner, stepped to the microphone to introduce the members of our Super Bowl team. His voice was softer than usual. Even his smile was softer.

"This is truly an emotional and inspirational experience, to be here tonight," Al said. "This morning I called this great class of '76 one of the greatest football teams of all time. To break bread with them, to see their faces, and to remember them as if it were only yesterday, these are the things you love about professional football, and you love being part of the Raiders."

At the brunch, Al had remembered how he once had been asked to introduce the Raider team, not long after we had won Super Bowl XI, but he had declined "because I was signing all those guys and paying them." But up at the microphone now, Al couldn't wait to start introducing the Super Bowl players, plus a few other famous Raiders who had been invited to attend the reunion. "Tonight it's going to be a little easier," he continued. "We can give 'em all the love and emotion that we want."

Al introduced Clemon Daniels, a running back who helped turn the franchise around in 1963 after Al took over as the coach and general manager. He introduced Marv Hubbard, Raymond Chester, and Rod Sherman.

Then Al said, "In 1967 I had just got done telling Tom

Flores that he'd be with us for life. But then somebody from the Buffalo Bills called and said, 'Would you be interested in Daryle Lamonica?' I said, 'Very much so.' He said, 'We'd be interested in Tom Flores as part of the deal.' I then determined that Tom Flores would not be with us for life. But it was our good fortune at that time to get, from the University of Notre Dame, as good a deep passer as this game has ever seen: the Mad Bomber, Daryle Lamonica."

Everybody in the audience applauded, as they had for each of the players Al had introduced.

"I'm not a master of ceremonies, and never have been," Al said, "but they told me to please ask you not to applaud until we've introduced all the players. And if you do, we'll fine you. We don't collect the fines, though. We never did. But before we go on, I want to tell you this story about the great John Madden. The rumor was all over the world that *I* was the guy who used to hold back the films from the other teams, that I never sent the films on time. John was sending the films, but John was the good guy, and I was orchestrating John. Well, we were playing Miami and John pulls a fast one. He switches the film. He doesn't send it late, he sends some other game instead of the game he's supposed to send.

"On the field before the game, John meets the Dolphins coach, the late George Wilson, and George said, 'John, that goddamn Al Davis sent us the wrong film,' and John said, 'I don't know what the hell's wrong with Al, I've been telling him not to do those things.' "

In the laughter, Al said, "The only difference between me and the other roasters, I'm telling the truth." Then he introduced "the greatest clutch player who ever played professional football—George Blanda," and "the next guy,

I remember putting his picture and George Blanda's picture on a poster together because they always symbolized in my mind a commitment to excellence, pride, and poise: the indestructible Double Zero—Jim Otto." Then he introduced Ray Guy, our Super Bowl punter, who had been the Raiders' first-round choice in the 1973 draft.

"The greatest punter of all time, I don't think anyone can dispute it," Al said. "We had the greatest players. We had the greatest coaches. We were the most feared, the most intimidating.

"The kicker on that team was Errol Mann," Al said, introducing our place kicker from that season. "I wanted to go to the quarterback next, but I want to talk about another quarterback we had who exemplifies everything we believe in . . . that there is a will, that there is a way to come back, that it isn't always over when things are tough. That's why I think the Raiders have always been tough late in the football game. Here's the winner of two Super Bowls for the Raiders later on, the great Jim Plunkett."

After the applause, Al chuckled and looked over at where Ray Guy was standing in his tuxedo.

"When I see Ray in a tuxedo," Al said, laughing, "I get a thrill, because I never thought I'd ever be in one either. And John Madden in a tuxedo. You're laughing, but wait'll I tell you the first time I met John Madden. I'd come to Oakland as head coach and general manager. I didn't know John Madden, but in the papers was a statement that we were looking for a training site for our summer camp. That's when I found the great camp in Santa Rosa— a hotel, football fields, good food. We had negotiated down to $8.35 a day for room and board.

"But then I got a phone call one day from the guy who

was the head coach at Allan Hancock Junior College. He introduced himself as John Madden. He wanted us to come to his college.

"I told him I was all set, I just got a beautiful place up in Santa Rosa—three meals a day, steak, all the good food, a low price, everything. John told me had just been to see his president. He could get it for five dollars a day. He told us he could bunk four in a room. He wanted us there. But that was all on the phone. I never met John Madden until 1966. I was scouting San Diego State, where he was an assistant coach. I can only describe him to you. He was standing on that football field wearing high-cleat shoes, almost up above his ankle. Baggy football pants. A jacket that must've come from a rummage sale. And a hat, a baseball cap. And he was pretty fancy, because he had a whistle on.

"But goddamn, when I talked to him, I felt an emotional love for football. Something about him was a little different than those you come across from time to time. So in 1967 he came to the Raiders. In 1969 at the age of thirty-two, he was made the head coach. And I don't have to tell you about the records. We've heard about 'em tonight.

"I thought there was something great in the little brochure that was given to us tonight. Someone wrote that John and the Oakland Raiders were more than just a football team. They were, for him and for many of us who proudly wore the silver, the black, the epitome of pride and poise, a team that played pro football with complete abandon simply because they loved the game."

One by one, Al resumed introducing other Super Bowl XI players from our 1976 team. About the next guy, he said, "From the word go, he liked to have fun. I knew we could never totally control him, but I also had the gut feeling that no one who played against him would be able to control him either. He's probably the most accurate passer of all time, Kenny 'The Snake' Stabler." Then he went on, giving a short description of each player.

"He rushed for a hundred thirty-nine yards in that Super Bowl—Clarence Davis. . . . A brilliant fullback, a great guy—Mark Van Eeghen. . . . A guy who was captain at Notre Dame, and *how* he was captain at Notre Dame I'll never understand—Dave Casper. . . . The left tackle, he'll be a Hall of Famer—Art Shell. . . . He wasn't a tough guy, we had to make him tough. He played forever, the only guy who played in a Super Bowl in the 1960's, the 1970's, *and* the 1980's—Gene Upshaw. . . . He only played fifteen years, great leadership, great center—Dave Dalby. . . . We got him as a tight end, he didn't want to play for us as a lineman, he thought he was Stanford and the line would be degrading to his mentality, a great guard—George Buehler. . . . A great pass-protector at right tackle. We had to play the Pittsburgh Steelers and we had to have someone who would match up with L. C. Greenwood—we had the right guy—John Vella. . . . A guy who played a great part in our Super Bowl victory, Minnesota had a great player in their goal-line defense that we were going to run at. He took care of him so Pete Banaszak could cross that goal line—Henry Lawrence. . . . A little wide receiver who put the fear of God in every team we played—Cliff Branch.

"On defense, truly a great player—Otis Sistrunk. . . . We traded for this guy, the nose guard—Dave Rowe."

When his name was called, each player walked up onto the stage, but they kept changing places in the line.

"They *still* don't know where to line up," Al said now, turning back to the microphone after motioning to the players behind him. "The next guy, who literally couldn't get along in other organizations, and I'm not sure he got along in ours—John Matuszak. . . . A great linebacker from that Super Bowl team—Monte Johnson. . . . In 1971 we thought we had lost a little toughness, so in the draft we said 'we're going for the toughest guys.' Our second-round choice was out of Bowling Green, and tough. I remember sitting in my living room one year, and this guy gets on and starts talking about the Raiders, how we play tough football, how we smashed you, that's the Raider way. A great tough player—Phil Villapiano."

Phil hurried up onto the stage, but instead of letting Phil get in line with the other players behind him, Al stepped back slightly. "Phil," he said, "I'd like you to take the microphone for thirty seconds. I'd like you to tell the crowd the story of the great trade."

Phil wasn't bashful. "I would love to do this," he said in his husky voice. "I've been waiting to tell this story. I was in New Jersey, and it was a beautiful spring morning, and I got up and went to church at seven o'clock mass, and I was going to come home and lift weights because I was getting ready for the 1981 season, because they put me in the middle. Me, a middle linebacker. I said I was going to be two hundred twenty-one pounds instead of two hundred twenty, I was going to be big enough to play the middle. Now, the phone rings. At nine o'clock in the morning, it's six o'clock in Oakland, but Al used to call me and talk about football, and I always thought that was great.

"He'd pump me for information—how was Ditka when he was at Dallas, could he play anymore? I said, 'He stunk.' Things like that. He'd ask me about Conrad Dobler and I'd make a good comment about how bad he was.

"And now, on the phone that Sunday morning, Al said, 'Phil, there's a guy up in Buffalo, a great receiver, his name is Bobby Chandler. What do you think?' I said, 'Bobby Chandler? He caught eight passes against us in that Monday night game in '74. I think he's a great player. I'd go get him, man.' Al said, 'Yeah, Phil, I think we can get him,' and I said, 'Who do we have to give?' and Al said, 'You.'

"I said, 'Al, am I gone?' He said, 'You're gone, man.' My good friend sent me to Buffalo, but they paid me more money in Buffalo than I ever got in Oakland."

Phil stepped back from the microphone and Al laughed. "That's why Phil called me every night for about two years to bring him back," Al said, smiling. "He should've played better the year before. . . . Now, the next guy, the Raiders gave two first-round draft choices for, we over-paid him, but we're not going to give him the micro-phone—the great Ted Hendricks." And as Ted passed behind me, he handed me a little teddy bear.

"We're paying the guy four hundred thousand a year," Al said, "and he gives John a teddy bear. When the secre-taries used to come in and say, 'Mr. Davis, Ted Hendricks is on the phone,' I'd say, 'Keep him on the phone. At least we know where he is.' . . . The next guy, we called him Doctor Death—the great Alonzo (Skip) Thomas. . . . A little fellow we got from Morris Brown in 1968. He wanted a six-thousand dollar bonus, which was a lot of money in those days. I said, 'Get him signed for five years and give him seven thousand.' They did that, but in a year or two he was in asking for a renegotiation: George Atkin-son. . . . In 1971 we wanted toughness, the guy we took as number one was tough. To this day he's the guy who sets the standard of excellence for toughness in the secondary—Jack Tatum. . . . This guy was from Grambling University, and I think he's the greatest player to have ever played his position of cornerback—Willie Brown.

"And of course, the great head coach of that 1976 season, I'm very proud to introduce a guy I love, a great friend. Let's have a hand for a great guy—John Madden."

I'd been sitting there listening and laughing for about two hours, but now it was the roastee's turn to have fun. I stood up and talked about how Parris Farzar had suggested a roast, but I'd already been roasted. How he wanted to have a birthday party. But how when he mentioned that it would be the tenth anniversary reunion for our Super Bowl team, I had agreed.

"You go through life," I said now, "and people say, 'What was the greatest highlight?' and the greatest highlight was the Super Bowl—not just winning the game, not just having a ring, not just the money, but doing it with these people.

"Football was fun then. I get the idea now, I'm sure Mike Ditka will agree, that sometimes these players now don't have any fun. I mean, they've got agents and lawyers. But these guys here tonight, they didn't know any better. They'd come in—gimme a job, where do I line up, who do I hit? These guys up here, weren't they beauties? They had a helluva time filling up this table, trying to get these guys to dress up in a tuxedo and let people watch 'em eat.

"We said we had pride, we had poise. You never heard us say we were smart. No one ever accused us of being smart.

"Upshaw used to hold. He couldn't block, so he'd hold. He would tape his hands all the way up the arm, with white tape. Now we'd go to play the Pittsburgh Steelers.

He's blocking Ernie Holmes—*boom,* the official sees the white tape on the black jersey. So I said, 'If you're going to hold, you can't hold with white tape on a black jersey. You got to put shoe polish on it and make it black, then when you hold, you got black holding black and they can't see it.'

"Upshaw thought, 'This is a smart coach.' The next time he gets a holding penalty, he says, 'I didn't hold him.' I say, 'Why'd he call it then?' He says, 'I don't know, he's blind, I didn't hold the guy.' The next day I looked at the film. Upshaw had him with both hands, arms, up, down, face-mask, everything. I thought, *I can't wait to get this guy.*

"Upshaw comes in and I'm ready for him. I said, 'Hey, listen, you said you didn't hold, but it was terrible, it was brutal. I saw it on film. I'm going to show it to everyone.' And he said, 'Did you want Snake to get killed?' Now what the hell do you do? I got Snake out there, he looks bad. That's why we never ran on the field. We'd come out on the field, we didn't run, we just walked. If you had to run, the other team would look at number twelve and they'd laugh. Skinny legs, bad knees, he couldn't run. So when Upshaw said, 'Did you want Snake to get killed?' I said, 'No, I don't want Snake killed.' He didn't say, 'Do you want to take a sack,' because I might say, 'Yeah, I want to take a sack.' No, he said, 'Did you want Snake to get killed?' I said, 'No.' Then he said, 'OK, if I don't hold that guy, he was going to kill Snake.'

"Upshaw's got me, and that's bad enough, but now he goes out and tells all the offensive linemen. George Buehler, he'll believe anything. Art Shell, Dave Dalby, John Vella, Henry Lawrence. He tells 'em, 'John says it's OK to hold.' He's giving speeches behind my back to the team. They say, 'Is that right, Gene?' He says, 'Yeah, we got to protect Snake, we can hold if we have to. Whatever it takes.' Now *this* guy is leading the Players Association."

That's the fun of a roast. At the end, the roastee has the opportunity to roast the roasters.

"Mike Ditka," I said now. "I'm sure there are psychologists, psychiatrists, who can figure this out. Mike Ditka, great player, great coach. He breaks his hand punching a locker, so the next game he wears a necktie."

"That was the cast," Mike piped up from his seat. "That was the cast I wore."

"You told me you wore the necktie so you wouldn't hit anything," I said.

"That was a couple weeks later."

"Yeah, because you got so emotional. Mike Ditka always wears a necktie now, because he doesn't want to get emotional anymore."

"It works," Mike said.

"Jim Tunney, the referee," I said. "Who the hell put him next to me? I hate officials. I don't know how you guys get to be referees. I never heard of a kid growing up wanting to be an official. Where do these guys come from? Who are you guys? Have you ever heard in school, 'What do you want to be when you grow up?' They want to be firemen. They want to be policemen. They want to be astronauts. But who the hell ever wanted to be an official? Where do these guys come from? No one likes 'em. They get booed.

"But we had great fans in Oakland, we really did. I remember Don Shula in a league meeting getting up and saying, 'We have to do something about fan control. The worst fans in the NFL are in Oakland. Those people are right behind your bench, they're throwing stuff. You go out there and you don't know if you're going to get away with your life.'

"I'm sitting there in the meeting. I always had a couple of good deals. I had one in Al Davis. I mean, whatever happened, I'd say stuff like, 'I agree with you, but you know that goddamn Al, he waters the field, he does this, he does that.' And now I thought, *Do I agree with Shula?* I agreed with him. I raised my hand and said, 'That's right, those people are crazy. We have no control over 'em.' I said, 'When you bring your team in there, I don't know what's going to happen. I can't guarantee any safety over there. We try, we just don't know what to do. The stands come right down to the bench. We just can't do anything about these people.'

"Then I'd go back to Oakland and say, 'We have the greatest fans in the world' and they'd be yelling, 'Yay, yay, yay, the Raiders.' It was great. But even more important than that, it was fun.

"The other thing is charity. I want to thank all you people for coming here tonight. We're going to do something with this money. It's not going to be anything that just starts somewhere and filters down. It's going to go right where it's needed. And basically, I think it's needed with kids.

"We go around and we say, 'Well, when I was a kid . . .' Hey, it's a different ballgame out there now. When someone used to do something bad, they drank a beer or they went behind a barn and smoked. But it didn't kill anyone.

"Now these guys got stuff out in the street that can kill you. It's part of what we have to do. To give back. To get it before it starts. To give kids a chance. And we're going to do it with what we have here. We're going to help kids. And if this saves some lives, then we can all stand up and shake our own hands."

As much as I enjoyed the evening, I think Al Davis enjoyed it more than anybody else. Al usually has the look of a person who's got a problem. That's because he's usually *got* a problem. But in the lobby, later, Al was still hanging around, talking to everybody, laughing, not wanting the evening to end. He was still there when I went up to get out of my tuxedo.

I'M AN EX-COACH

I stopped coaching the Raiders after the 1978 season. That's a long time ago. But people are still asking me, "Will you ever coach in the NFL again?" All sorts of people ask me that all the time. Strangers in the street. Fans at games. Sportswriters. Sometimes even executives of NFL clubs.

My answer is, "No."

Over the years, nearly a dozen NFL teams have sounded me out on coaching again, but it was never the owner of any of those clubs who phoned. Usually it was a friend of the owner, or someone down the ladder in the organization. I've even been contacted about a college coaching job. It's always flattering to get that phone call, but I've given everybody the same answer.

"Thanks for thinking of me," I'd say, "but I'm not interested."

I doubt if I will ever be interested. Never say never. But when I got those phone calls, I didn't ask how much they were offering, or how long the contract was for. If you wanted to be coaxed into coaching, those are the first things you'd find out, then you'd say something like, "I'm really not interested, but let me think about it," which means you really *are* interested. But when all you say is "No," period, they know you mean it.

It's easy for me to mean it. I'm making a lot more money as an ex-coach than I ever did as a coach. And by the time I stopped coaching the Raiders, coaching was out of my system. I'd done it, and I didn't want to do it anymore.

I never really recovered from winning Super Bowl XI with my 1976 Raider team. After all those seasons of trying to win the Super Bowl, I had finally done it. But then I knew that all I could do was win it again. If it hadn't been for a bad call in the 1977 AFC championship game in Denver, I think we would've won Super Bowl XII too. But that just reminded me how difficult it is to win the Super Bowl, and when we struggled through the 1978 season, I decided that was it.

I had an ulcer that 1978 season, but the ulcer wasn't the reason I stopped coaching. Lots of people with ulcers work at their jobs.

The reason was, I just didn't want to coach anymore. Sooner or later, every coach feels that way. Tom Landry, who has coached the Dallas Cowboys ever since the team was organized in 1960, has told me, "I'll retire when I don't look forward to training camp anymore." But he's had more staying power than I did. I stopped looking forward to training camp after the 1978 season. Nobody in the NFL believed me. They thought I wanted to get away from Al Davis or they thought I wanted a change of scenery. That's why so many people sounded me out. *He doesn't want to coach,* they were thinking, *but I'll get him.* I've often thought that if somebody wanted a better job—not just a coaching job, but any job—the way to do it would be to quit their job, say they didn't want to do it anymore, and then wait for people to coax them into coming back to take a better one.

The way things worked out, most people assume that I had the Miller Lite commercials and my CBS job lined up. All I really had lined up was the idea that I'd try to work with my friend Jim Lange in real estate. My first day, I stood on line at City Hall in Pleasanton to get a sewer permit for a shopping mall. My real-estate career opened and closed with one sewer permit.

If the Miller Lite commercials and my CBS job hadn't developed, I might have gone back to coaching in a year or two, but I never wanted to be the general manager of an NFL team. The general manager has a frustrating job. I'd want either to be in control of the game as the coach, or not to be there at all. As the general manager, you're responsible for what the team does, but you don't have any control over what happens in the game. One way or another, I'm sure I would've stayed in pro football. I might have pursued a feeler from Commissioner Pete Rozelle to work out of the NFL office. But if I had to guess, I probably would have wound up being a radio analyst on Raider games.

In my travels now, some NFL coaches have asked me how I handled the ebb and flow of coaching. Not that I'm a career counselor for coaches. I don't think an NFL coach has ever made a career decision based on what I told him.

But for any coach, I think it boils down to whether you still look forward to coaching. If you do, keep coaching. If you don't, stop.

Hey, the way I look at it, I'm lucky I was a football coach. Not because I was successful. Not because one of my Raider teams won the Super Bowl. Not because it provided me with an identity that has carried over to my job as a TV analyst and to my commercials. I'm lucky because the more I think about it, the more I realize that football is the only sport I *could* have coached.

I guess I could've learned enough about other sports, but with my size, I couldn't have dressed the part.

I can't imagine myself in a baseball dugout as a manager, wearing one of those tight-fitting double-knit uniforms with knickers, colored stockings, and a silly little cap on my head.

I can't imagine myself in a boxing ring, wearing a satin jacket and carrying a bucket. Imagine me just trying to climb through the ropes!

I can't imagine myself as a pro basketball coach, conforming to the NBA's dress code of jacket and tie. I remember a playoff game in the Boston Garden when Pat Riley, the Lakers' coach, sweated right through his jacket. But he never took it off.

I can't imagine myself sitting in the stands in tennis, where a coach can't even talk to his player.

Most of all, I can't imagine myself as an Olympic diving coach, wearing a little Speedo bikini.

But as a football coach, I wore what I wanted. I didn't have to carry a bucket. I was able to talk to my players. And after ten seasons, I got it out of my system. It's still out.

I'LL NEVER RETIRE

s great as the bus is, some of the CBS guys won't ride in it with me except on short trips, from Washington or Philadelphia back to New York, after a Sunday game. They never come on the long overnight trips.

"I've got all those frequent flyer plans," one of them told me. "I don't get mileage with you."

"Madden Miles," another suggested. "If you had a Madden Miles deal, we'd ride the bus with you."

That's all those guys think about, frequent flyer miles. But hey, *one* guy who flies appreciates my bus. The time

I did the Space Agency public-service spot with Chuck Yeager, that was all he wanted to talk about. After we taped the spot in Sunnyvale, California, there was Chuck Yeager, the Air Force pilot who broke the sound barrier in 1947 in the X-1 rocket research plane, now a retired brigadier general, checking out my bus.

"I've got a thirty-one-foot motor home," he said, "but I've always wanted a bus."

"It makes pretty good time," I said. "We went from San Francisco to New York in about fifty-six hours."

"I did that once in about an hour."

He wasn't bragging. He wasn't trying to impress me. And he wasn't trying to put down the bus.

"About an *hour?*" I said.

"Yeah. The SR-Seventy-one goes about twenty-three hundred miles an hour. It only takes you about an hour to go across the country."

"If I knew I could get there that fast," I said, "I'd be willing to try it."

"It's so hot in the cockpit at Mach II, you need a refrigerated flying suit. And you've got to start slowing down about three hundred fifty miles away from where you're going to land. If you didn't, you'd break all the windows in the houses."

"That's the way to get across the country," I said.

"I once drove straight across the country," Chuck said. "My pal Bud Anderson and I once took turns, driving from Wright Field in Ohio to Edwards Air Force Base in California, when there were just roads, no Interstate highways. We did it in forty-three hours, in a 1947 Buick Roadmaster that had those four holes on the side of each front fender. That was long before air-conditioning. If we were hot and saw a river or a lake, we'd stop, put on our swim trunks, and jump in."

"I can do that in my shower," I said. "I just don't like to let my feet get off the ground."

He looked down and grinned. "With those big feet," he said, winking, "I can understand why."

For several years, Chuck Yeager had been one of those guys I wanted to meet, to hang out with, and here we were kidding each other like we had been friends for years. I've been lucky. One way or another, I've met most of the sports people I've wanted to meet, usually at the Miller Lite reunions. Now, I also get to meet people in other fields.

Another guy who fascinated me was Donald Trump, the New York real-estate zillionaire. Around the time he bought the New Jersey Generals of the USFL, Virginia and I were in Wolf's Delicatessen on Fifty-seventh Street. We were waiting for our corned-beef sandwiches, not paying any attention to the other people who were coming and going. Suddenly, a tall blond guy in a pin-striped gray suit stopped at our table.

"John Madden," he said, "I'm Donald Trump."

His wife Ivana was with him and we asked them to sit with us. I couldn't get over it. Here was this guy with a zillion dollars having dinner with his wife in a New York deli.

"It's one of our favorite restaurants," he said.

The more Donald talked, the more he reminded me of Al Davis—so much so it almost was scary. The same searching tone in his voice. The same quick mind. And more than anything else, the same curiosity about everything. You would think Donald Trump would be talking all the time. Instead, he was listening. He would ask me a question and then he'd really listen.

"Now that I'm buying the Generals," he asked me, "what should I know?"

"Your most important person," I told him, "is your player-personnel director."

That seemed to surprise him. He had probably assumed that the coach or the general manager would be the most important person he had to hire. But the player-personnel director recommends the players.

"If he picks the right players," I explained, "you'll have a good team. If not, you won't."

Donald looked at me in the same way Al Davis used to look at me when I was the Raiders' coach, listening and thinking. Since our conversation that night, I've seen Donald occasionally. Whenever I read about him putting together another zillion-dollar deal, I can't fathom how he manages not only to get the deal done, but to get the buildings put up—buildings like his Trump Tower on Fifth Avenue, his Grand Hyatt Hotel on Forty-second Street, next to Grand Central Terminal. And his Atlantic City casino-hotels.

One of these days, I'd like to take Donald Trump on my bus, sit for a few hours, and really talk to him about how he does what he does.

The one person I haven't met but who I'd really like to talk to is Johnny Carson. To be so good for so long on television, he really has to be brilliant. Maybe a few people are tired of him, but not many. Not me, I know that. And being in television myself, I've begun to think about what *I'll* be doing in fifteen or twenty years. One thing's for sure, I know I'll never retire. I don't have a hobby to retire to, and it's too late for me to develop one. I can't see myself collecting stamps. If you don't develop a hobby like that when you're young, you never do. When I was young, I played football in the football season, I played basketball in the basketball season, I played baseball in the baseball season, and then I was ready to play football again in the next football season.

That's great when you're young. But when you get older, there's no carry-over. When you're thirty-five or forty-five, you can't suddenly start playing football. Sure, you can start playing golf or tennis or racquetball at that age, or you can jog. But when I was growing up, those were considered sissy sports.

I like to play golf now, but it's too late for me to be a really good golfer. I swim when I'm home in California, but I'm not exactly a candidate to win an Olympic medal. So in fifteen or twenty years, I expect to be still doing pretty much what I'm doing now. I learned in 1979 after I stopped coaching that I can't retire. Some people can retire to puttering in the garden or refinishing antiques or working a computer, but I won't. I wouldn't enjoy it. I'll never retire. In a few years, I'll probably cut back on my schedule, but I'll just keep doing what I'm doing.

One way or another, I'll always have a football season.

ABOUT THE
AUTHORS

JOHN MADDEN is a commentator for CBS on its Sunday NFL games. Once the head coach of the Oakland Raiders for ten seasons, he lives in California and New York with his wife, Virginia, and their two sons, Mike and Joe.

DAVE ANDERSON, a Pulitzer Prize-winning sports columnist for *The New York Times,* is the author of seventeen books. He lives in Tenafly, New Jersey, with his wife, Maureen. They have four children—Stephen, Mark, Mary Jo, and Jean Marie.